CW00839652

A Systematic Guide to Business Acumen and Leadership using Dilemmas

Includes Organizational Health, Agility, Resilience and Crisis Management

by

Ken Thompson

February 2016

REVISION: 1.10U

A Systematic Guide to Business Acumen
and Leadership using Dilemmas

A Systematic Guide to Business Acumen and Leadership using Dilemmas

A Systematic Guide to Business Acumen and Leadership

"We have used the thinking in this book to build business acumen training for our HR people – with tremendous success. The confidence they gain through using these concepts, delivered through highly realistic business simulations, has transformed the way they think about their businesses, and the contribution they are able to make".

DES PULLEN, Group HR Director, Associated British Foods

"Ken Thompson, in creating this valuable guide, highlights the key practical choices faced by managers in driving business performance. Ken has also assembled a portfolio of tools – drawn from his own experience as well as from global thought-leaders – that will help aspiring leaders, when push comes to shove, to make the right calls".

JAMES BOWEN, Managing Director of Kotinos Partners Limited, Performance Transformation specialists

"Often, when faced with a real dilemma, leaders show a bias for acting above thinking. Ken's book will help them adopt the optimum actions without overly complex analysis. A practical and reliable guide when the pressure is really on"!

ROB WIRSZYCZ, Chairman, advisor and mentor to businesses ranging from start-ups to publicly quoted

A Systematic Guide to Business Acumen and Leadership using Dilemmas

"In a true strategic decision 'the opposite' should also be an equally valid strategic option". Ken Thompson has taken this core thesis and extrapolated it into ten core dilemmas that will guide you in challenging your status quo. An ideal companion piece to Blue Ocean Strategy Canvas work".

PAUL SWEENEY, Product, innovation and change executive for start-ups.

A Systematic Guide to Business Acumen and Leadership using Dilemmas

Contents

About the Author

The book is authored by Ken Thompson who is an expert practitioner, author and speaker on collaboration, high performing teams, change management and game-based learning.

Ken has written a number of books and his work has featured in major publications including The Guardian Newspaper, Wired Magazine, The Huffington Post and The Henry Ford Magazine.

Ken has also spoken at a number of international events including TEDx, the Institute for Healthcare Improvement (IHI) and NASA conferences.

Introduction

Systematic Guides are aimed at leaders and managers who need to instantly access 'Organization-Ready' models, practices, checklists and guidance in key subject areas which are logically organized and based on best practice.

Each Systematic Guide references online team-based business simulation games, designed by the author, which provide powerful experiential and social learning tools for rapidly bringing each book's content to life in a fun and engaging way.

This guide offers a unique and concise review of ten very common types of business and leadership dilemma which leaders and managers face in major organizations. It is based on ten years' worth of interviewing, testing, and running simulation games with hundreds of subject matter experts, top performers, leaders, and managers across many different industries in my privileged role as a business simulation game designer.

The purpose of the guide is to equip new leaders to recognize these dilemmas whenever they first occur and be ready with strategies and tactics for dealing with them in a more masterful way to achieve results which go beyond the norm.

As well as preparing prospective Business Unit Leaders, the guide also serves as a 'Business Acumen Primer' for anyone who needs a broad overview of the types of challenges facing business unit leaders today. Thus the guide is highly relevant to young managers, 'high potentials', 'emerging talent' and, of course, HR and L&D professionals.

Based on my experience from collecting the dilemmas I propose a direct link between entrepreneurial dilemma resolution and high performance in business units.
I then propose a simple systematic approach for what it means to creatively explore and resolve such dilemmas.

As we navigate the ten dilemmas we also naturally encounter a number of important issues which business leaders are grappling with today including *Organizational Health, Agility, Resilience, Crisis Management* and *Organizational Mindfulness.*

Other books in The Systematic Guides series

A Systematic Guide to High Performing Teams (HPTs), Ken Thompson, December 2015

A Systematic Guide to Game-Based Learning (GBL) in Organizational Teams, Ken Thompson, January 2016

A Systematic Guide to Change Management, Ken Thompson, July 2016

Dilemma Resolution and High Performance

Over the last 10 years I have had the privilege of working closely with subject matter experts and high performers in major enterprises to design custom business simulation games to exactly match their organizational learning needs.

My discussions mostly concentrated on the key things which top performers did differently than others in their organizations to achieve their results. As these conversations developed I became increasingly aware that despite the amazing diversity of these businesses and the individuals who excelled in them there seemed to be a common theme.

Over and over again it appeared that top performers took a totally different approach to problems. Let me be more specific – when faced with a dilemma they usually rejected the obvious responses for something a bit more thoughtful, entrepreneurial and creative.

A dilemma is a values conflict requiring a choice. It usually requires some kind of trade-off between two (or more) things which you would like to protect or achieve. The difference between a dilemma and a decision is that there is always some pain or loss in a dilemma *at the point of decision-making*.

Let me give you an example. I have a friend; let's call him Graham, whose company designs board games for business. Think Monopoly but for business-based experiential learning. Graham's company is very successful and has grown its business internationally.

Out of the blue Graham discovered that an overseas company was manufacturing a complete copy of one of their popular board games but translated into the local language and culture.

This presented Graham with a dilemma. On one hand his intellectual property was being badly abused (Value 1: IP Protection) but on the other hand this overseas company clearly valued Graham's Products (Value 2: Business Opportunity). As they say, 'imitation is the sincerest form of flattery'.

What would you do?

A knee-jerk response would be a firm but courteous 'desist and refrain' letter with the implied threat of legal redress.

Graham considered this option but realized that any legal response would probably be impossible given the geography and the different attitude to intellectual property in the home country of the overseas company.

Graham decided instead to contact the company in a very positive way and to try to sell all the advantages of being a 'legit' supplier. This included Train the Trainer, Product Updates and Website marketing. As a result, Graham was able to turn the company not just into an official supplier but into one of his largest international suppliers.

This is an example of creative dilemma resolution (in this case super-imposed on top of two competing cultural systems). This is the kind of creativity that I saw over and over again in my conversations with high performers. (If you would like to explore creative cross-cultural dilemma resolution in detail I would refer to Fons Trompenaar's excellent book [1]).

So I my first contention is that top performers react to dilemmas in a different way than others.

However, I have a second contention: based on my conversations there also seems to be a common set of dilemma types which occur over and over again for those charged with leading business units.

I have been able to identify 10 dilemma types which broadly fall into two categories – Business Dilemmas and Leadership Dilemmas. However please don't take this classification too rigidly. As you will see there will always be overlap between the categories.

Business Dilemmas (1-5) mostly concern the operation of the whole business unit. **Leadership Dilemmas** (6-10) mostly concern the operation of the executive team leading the business unit.

Note that the 5 business dilemmas will vary in detail depending on the type of business. For example, in a digital business the Supply-Demand Dilemma might be more about human resources than external suppliers. The 5 leadership dilemmas, however, are more generic and more likely to arise in a similar form in any type of business.

The 10 dilemmas types are summarized in the figure below:

This book is dedicated to exploring each one of the ten dilemmas in turn, in detail.

FURTHER READING on Dilemmas

1. Did the Pedestrian Die, Fons Trompenaars, Capstone; March 2003

Creative Dilemma Resolution

Before we jump into each dilemma it is worth briefly
looking at the dilemma resolution process itself.

To creatively respond to a dilemma is not particularly
difficult PROVIDED you take the time to think it through
and not just make a knee-jerk response.

Therein lies the problem as if we are facing these kinds of
dilemmas, it usually means we are holding organizational
leadership responsibilities where spare time is the last
thing we have.

To help I suggest overleaf a 7-step process for creative
dilemma resolution under pressure.

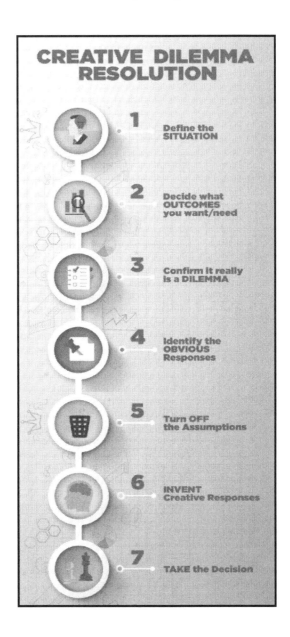

Let's look at each of the 7 steps in more detail:

1. Define the SITUATION
Which of your values does the situation set at odds? These are the 'horns' of the dilemma. In Graham's example it was IP Protection versus Business Opportunity. There are often also some 'Constraints' associated with a dilemma which restrict your freedom in terms of how you might respond. In Graham's case constraints would be around his personal time and access to/budget for high-powered IP lawyers with international reach.

2. Decide what OUTCOMES you want/need
Decide on your ideal outcome and your 'worst acceptable outcome' [1]. Your final chosen response should deliver something between these two extremes.

3. Confirm it really is a DILEMMA
If you can achieve your ideal outcome or close to it then good news – it's not a real dilemma. Go to Step 7.

4. Identify the OBVIOUS Responses
Now identify the obvious 'Knee-Jerk' responses to the situation and see how well any of them deliver your ideal outcome or close to it. If any of them do deliver this, then good news again – it's just a simple dilemma – no creativity required. Unless of course your 'Ideal Solution' lacks ambition – double check it! If it is good go to Step 7.

5. Turn OFF the Assumptions

What Assumptions are implicit in the dilemma within its Horns or its Constraints? What would change if you turned any of them off? For example, one of the constraints of your dilemma could be to operate within your agreed budgetary and resourcing levels. What if you could have additional budget and/or resources – could you achieve your ideal solution? If 'yes' then can you make a business case argument for flexing your budget or resources? If this resolves it for you then 'Good News' – go to Step 7.

6. INVENT Creative Responses

If you are at this step if means you have a non-simple dilemma for which you must generally accept the set of assumptions which are part of it. Now you need to be more creative and come up with some novel responses. One thing you can do here is to think about the whole question of TIME. For example, in Graham's case he wanted to *ultimately* address both values (IP and Business Opportunity) but he realized that if he started with the IP problem then he would be unlikely to ever get what he wanted. So in a sense he 'suspended' one of his values for a limited time but with a commitment to come back to it within a certain period. So you need to brainstorm some creative responses – perhaps with help from some innovative colleagues.

7. TAKE the Decision

Now you need to select the creative response which gets you closest to your ideal outcome and then monitor it carefully to see if it does in fact deliver your ideal outcome and if it might need to be tweaked.

FURTHER READING on Creative Dilemma Resolution

1. *Getting to Yes: Negotiating Agreement Without Giving In*, Roger Fisher and William Ury, Penguin Books, 1983

The TEN Dilemmas Summarized

1. *The Customer Dilemma* is primarily about how we decide which customers (or prospective customers) are most important at which times and how we might win their loyalty.

2. *The Product Dilemma* is essentially about how we optimize the contributions of our whole portfolio of product across their full lifetimes and how/when old products get retired and new products introduced.

3. *The Price Dilemma* concerns how we use pricing to optimize the 'trinity' of profit, demand, and market share in different market conditions and how we price to support products appropriate to their potential and maturities.

4. *The Mix Dilemma* is fundamentally about how we mix (i.e. optimize) the different options available to us in terms of products, markets and other factors (such as supply, geography and currency) to produce the best business results at the lowest business risk.

5. *The Supply & Demand Dilemma* is primarily about how we strike a balance between having too much supply of our product (or its components) and having too little to satisfy our customer's demand and how we achieve this in the most profitable manner.

6. *The Planning Dilemma* is essentially about getting the right balance between developing comprehensive plans and mobilizing plans through conversations. It is also about how we avoid the artifacts of planning becoming ends in themselves.

7. *The Results dilemma* concerns how we design and effectively monitor a balanced set of measures which keep our' eyes on the prize' while providing us with effective tracking and early warning systems.

8. *The Health Dilemma* is primarily about how we strike a balance between delivering the required results today while protecting and enhancing the ability of our organization to deliver the results it needs in the future.

9. *The Agility Dilemma* is about our ability to respond effectively to and learn from all types of unexpected change both minor and major. It is also about how we design systems to warn of, build resilience to and respond to future shocks, so that if they cannot be avoided or absorbed at least we can manage them with less pain.

10. *The Team Dilemma* is how we balance the tensions between being an effective, autonomous and motivating leader with being a supportive and loyal member of a senior team.

EXERCISE

1. Refer to Appendix C for a full-page version of the ten central dilemmas.
2. Mark on it the essence of each dilemma ('the horns') <u>as it applies to your organization/role.</u>
3. Identify the 3 dilemmas which have the highest importance to your organization/role.
4. Have a session with your colleagues to generate ideas about how the relevant people in your organization might have more options at their disposal for creatively resolving each of them in the future.

Dilemma#1: Customer

The Customer Dilemma is primarily about how we decide which customers (or prospective customers) are most important at which times and how we might win their loyalty.

Before we look at customer dilemmas we need to briefly look at some important customer concepts.

Customer Loyalty

If your business is designed to encourage repeat business, which most are, your customers can be categorized according to their loyalty using a Customer Loyalty Ladder (aka Brand Funnel).

One of the simplest Loyalty Ladders is a 3 stage ladder:

- LOYALS (or FANS)
- REGULARS
- OCCASIONALS

Each of these customer groups will be characterized by different "Loyalty" measured in a number of ways including:

- Average Spend/Basket Size
- Frequency of Spend
- Net Promoter Score [1]

It would be quite common for LOYALS to have an Average Spend which is considerably higher than REGULARS which in turn would be considerably higher than OCCASIONALS.

Customer Drivers

These loyalty groupings are not static; companies are always trying to push customers 'up the loyalty ladder' and retain those at the higher levels. These efforts will be counteracted by negative forces and competitor activity working in the other direction to force customers down the ladder or off the ladder and onto somebody else's ladder ('switchers').

Typical Drivers for promoting and retaining customers with respect to the loyalty ladder include:

- Branding
- Marketing
- Sales
- Quality
- Innovation
- Customer Service

and, of course, Price which we will deal with in detail in the Price Dilemma chapter.

Market Share

Companies measure their market share in different ways.
'Wallet Share' is the percentage of the revenue you take
across your competitors. 'Volume Share' is the percentage
of the total customers you own across your competitors.
'Segment Share' is the percentage of a certain type of
customer you own compared with your competitors.

Customer Satisfaction

Customer Satisfaction is what I refer to as a 'Slow-Grow-
Quick-Fall' business indicator. In other words, like
reputation or trust, it can take a long time and a lot of
effort to build up but it can drop like a stone as an adverse
reaction to events. This results in customers dropping
down or dropping off your customer loyalty ladder.

The factors which impact customer satisfaction will vary
depending on the type of product or service and of course
your brand strength. Companies go to a lot of expense to
market research customer/consumer priorities in this
area.

Prospective Customers

Prospective Customers (or prospects) are those consumers
who are not currently your customers but who are open to
the possibility of becoming your customers. They can be
'Category Prospects' which means that they are currently
somebody else's customer for your type of product or
service.

They can also be 'Non-Category' Customers which means they don't currently use your specific type of product or service. For example, if your product is coffee then Non-Category could be consumers who prefer cold beverages or those who drink only tea.

Common Customer Dilemmas

Two common business dilemmas frequently result from the above:

Different Drivers affect Different Prospects and Customers

In one business I worked with, for them to win new customers for a specific product they had to make Marketing top priority and Sales second priority. However, to retain existing customers they had to make Sales top priority with Marketing second priority.

If you have limited resources and budget, then you have a dilemma!

Different Customer Groups affect Key Business Indicators

Let's say you are tasked with growing Sales Revenue and Market Share which on the face of it seems very reasonable and is in fact a key element of many business unit leaders' annual goals. When you clarify your objectives with your boss, as you should always do, you find out that it is the 'volume' kind of Market Share which is their priority.

You have a dilemma. To grow volume share you must concentrate on winning new customers, who, if you are successful, will join the loyalty ladder at the very bottom with the lowest average basket size and least revenue contribution.

However, to grow Sales Revenue you really should focus on the 'Regulars' and 'Loyals' who have the biggest basket sizes but who won't contribute any growth whatsoever to your volume market share. This is another classic Customer Dilemma.

Other Common Dilemmas

If you are in an early stage business or are introducing a new product to the market, then another customer dynamic can come into play.

Let's assume you don't yet have any customer loyalty for your new product or service (this is an over-simplification as you could have overarching brand loyalty which might encourage your customers for your other products to try your new product). Therefore, in this case, you need to think beyond the Customer Loyalty Ladder to the *Customer Adoption Cycle* which suggests that customers take 5 different attitudes towards adopting new products or services:

- INNOVATORS
- EARLY ADOPTERS

- EARLY MAJORITY
- LATE MAJORITY
- LAGGARDS

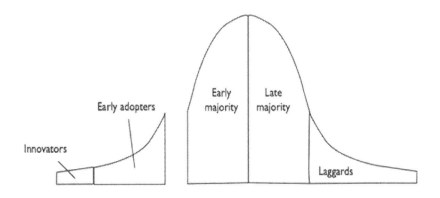

You would need to develop a strategy for getting each of these categories on board as customers starting with the Innovators and Early Adopters. However, the step between Early Adopter and Early Majority is known in the literature [2] as the Chasm because this is where another key dilemma occurs.

Many companies find it hard to cross this chasm. One frequently cited reason is that Innovators and Early Adopters distract the company with feedback which is not representative of the 3 later categories and thus stall the companies' general adoption plans.

The dilemma here could be articulated as when do you listen to your customers and when do you ignore them?

SELF-REFLECTION EXERCISE

1. *How/where does the 'Customer Dilemma' manifest itself most strongly in your organization or team?*

2. *Can you identify some recent examples where difficult choices had to be made around different types of Customer?*

3. *Can you select one of these examples and use the Creative Dilemma Resolution process to brainstorm an alternative response?*

FURTHER READING on Customer

1. *The Ultimate Question 2.0*, Fred Reichheld, Harvard Business School, Sept. 2011
2. *Crossing The Chasm: Marketing and Selling Disruptive Products to Mainstream Customers*, Geoffrey Moore, Harper Business, Dec. 2002

Dilemma#2: Product

The Product Dilemma is essentially about how we optimize the contributions of our whole portfolio of product across their full lifetimes and how/when old products get retired and new products introduced.

When we start to think about the product (including services) dilemma there are 4 important product-related topics we first need to appreciate some product concepts:

- Product Contributions
- Product Growth Potentials
- Product Lifecycles
- Product Innovation

The Product Dilemma is somewhat pervasive and therefore we will also visit it again in the chapters on Price and Mix dilemmas.

Product Contributions

Each product in your business has a worth or 'contribution'. There are 3 main ways you can measure its contribution – revenue, profit and 'other'.

Ideally you would like all your products to be high revenue and high profit but that will not always be possible.

Some products make a major contribution to revenue (high revenue share percentage) but are not very profitable when costs are taken into account. This might indicate a problem with the product ("the busy fool syndrome") or it might be that the product's market is so competitive and crowded that high profits are just not possible at this time.

It is important to remember that high revenue-low profit products can still make a very important contribution to covering the fixed costs of the business without which it might slip into losses.

Other products can have low revenue contribution but are very profitable and can make the difference between missing and achieving profit targets. Obviously you need to explore whether you can grow sales in this case, however sometimes, particularly in service businesses, there can be high profit opportunities which just arise from time to time. An example could be urgent customer changes being needed within the context of single supplier IT support contracts. In this case customers may have a weak negotiating position which suppliers can exploit with high prices and resulting profits.

The third type of product contributor is where the product has some other value. For example, products which allow customers to treat you as a one-stop shop rather than spilled supply. Another common example, loved by the supermarkets, is the loss-leader which brings people into the store. The equivalent of this on the service side is the "diagnostic audit" often offered free or highly subsidized which is designed to lead to subsequent full-fee consulting work.

Product Growth Potentials

Once you understand (and are happy with) a product's contribution you need to establish what its growth potential is. Aside from price which we discuss later there are 2 main ways to grow product revenue – market opportunities and time-critical opportunities.

In the first case, market opportunities, we are interested in the size of the market, whether it is growing or declining and the size of our market share relative to our competition. We should be asking ourselves whether we could take more market share, for example compared to the market share we enjoy for other comparable products?

In the second case, time-based opportunities, we will be looking at things like seasonality, weather, major events and market activity. For example, in terms of seasonality many retailers earn a disproportionate amount of their annual revenues in pre-Christmas sales during November and December.

In terms of weather we eat more curries and drink more tea when the weather is bad. In terms of major events the Soccer and Rugby World Cups and the Olympics results in more drinks and sales of television sets. In terms of market activity, a competitor product launch might energize a market and create new opportunities for our existing products as well, of course, as threats.

In both market-based and time-based growth opportunities we will be looking to support them through marketing and sales activities. This can raise some interesting 'ethical dilemmas'. For example, when a convenience store determines that cigarette sales are making a major contribution to both revenues and profits but also recognize that it may be ethically questionable to try to grow this revenue for example by in-store product placement.

Product Lifecycles

Every product or service can be thought of has having a natural lifecycle similar to the human cycle:

- NEW PRODUCT (child)
- GROWING PRODUCT (teenager)
- PRIME PRODUCT (adult)
- MATURE PRODUCT (middle age)
- DECLINING PRODUCT (senior)

We will talk more about Pricing Strategies at different stages in the product lifecycle in the Chapter on Pricing.

Another and more sophisticated way to look at the Product Lifecycle question is through the lens of the Boston Matrix/Grid [1].

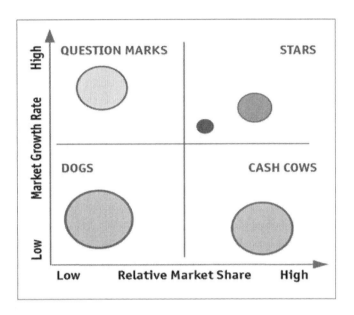

This approach categorizes products on two axes – Market Share and Market Growth - and results in 4 distinct product categories:

- CASH COW
- STAR
- QUESTION MARK
- DOG

A CASH COW has high market share but low market growth. Cash Cows are the foundation of successful companies with high profits and minimum investment required.

A STAR ticks both boxes – high market share and high growth but may not yet be generating strong revenues or profits because of the level of investment it currently needs. If carefully managed, Stars can become the future Cash Cows for the company.

A QUESTION MARK (aka PROBLEM CHILD) is the opposite of a Cash Cow with low market share but high market growth. Question Marks need to be invested in to see if they can become Cash Cows and if not then liquidated.

A DOG ticks neither box – it is a low market share and low growth proposition. If Dogs are not making minimum levels of profit, then they should be retired.

A key feature of the Boston Matrix is that nothing stays the same and if you are not actively managing and pruning your product set you will be in for a nasty surprise at some point.

If you can understand where each of your existing products is in terms of both its human lifecycle and its Boston Matrix position, then you are a good way towards developing an integrated 'portfolio' of products rather than just a random collection.

Product Innovation

A central product dilemma is when to introduce new products and when to retire old ones. Here I am talking about genuine new product designs rather than on-going product-line extensions which are designed to prolong the life of existing product designs.

For some businesses such as seasonal retail fashion the decision is already made for them as new products must be introduced <u>every single quarter</u> based on new fashion designs and outsourced manufacturing. Such products are relatively low risk in that all that is at stake is really just the number of units which can be sold in the quarter.

The dilemma is how much to make to avoid the 2 extremes of not being able to meet demand to having made too much product which you have to shift at heavy discount. Obviously the more you make the better the economies of scale on cost and thus profit, which makes the "how much to make" dilemma very interesting.

In other businesses, such as pharmaceuticals or software development companies, the question of the timing of innovation is a really big deal. This is because in these sectors new products may have development periods in the years or even tens of years. These products may require large R&D investments and multiple "gates" where the products can be culled to try and reduce the risk of bringing expensive failures to the market. Such R&D intensive enterprises must literally 'bet the business' on the success of their next major new product.

A very useful concept here is the 3 horizons of innovation model suggested by former McKinsey consultants in their book *The Alchemy of Growth* [2].

Horizon 1: EXISTING
Goal: Defend and Extend Current Core Businesses

Horizon 2: EMERGING
Goal: Build Momentum of Emerging New Businesses

Horizon 3: EMBRYONIC
Goal: Create Options for Future Businesses

The authors suggest it can typically take 3-5 years to successfully transition a product or set of related products to the next horizon depending on the industry sector.

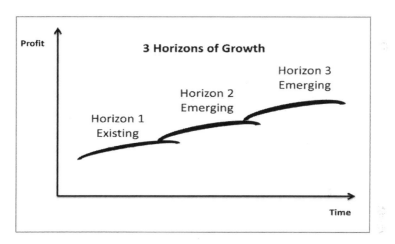

One of the most serious mistakes is when enterprises only really have an EXISTING Horizon Product Set. They can be very successful – until this Product Set is suddenly threatened by something unexpected! What they then have to do is to try and fast-track an EMBRYONIC Product Set into the EXISTING Horizon without going through the EMERGING Horizon.

This rarely succeeds and I have seen the effects first hand when consulting to a cables and components company who had not anticipated the impact of internet e-commerce of their business. The company tried (and failed) to rapidly catch up with competitors who had stolen a march on them. In this case they did not even have an EMERGING or EMBRYONIC Horizon Product Set and had to try to fast track an ENVISIONED Product Set which was little more than ideas and notes on a flip chart.

That in itself is another key point from *The Alchemy of Growth* book – an EMBRYONIC Product Set is a set of products which are actually in the market and earning some, albeit small revenues. A set of *PowerPoints* or even detailed designs or product prototypes is not an EMBRYONIC Product Set!

A truly innovative company will be managing all 3 horizons of products concurrently and not just focusing on their current business products. Such a company is automatically future-proofing itself by investing some profits today to secure profits in the future.

SELF-REFLECTION EXERCISE

1. *How/where does the 'Product Dilemma' manifest itself most strongly in your organization or team?*

2. *Can you identify some recent examples where difficult choices had to be made around Pricing?*

3. *Can you select one of these examples and use the Creative Dilemma Resolution process to brainstorm an alternative response?*

FURTHER READING on Product

1. *The Product Portfolio*, Bruce Henderson, www.bcgperspectives.com, 1970
2. *The Alchemy of Growth: Practical Insights for Building the Enduring Enterprise*, Baghai, Coley and White, Basic Books, 2000

Dilemma#3: Price

The Price Dilemma concerns how we use pricing to optimize the 'trinity' of profit, demand and market share in different market conditions and how we price to support products appropriate to their potential and maturities.

The Price Dilemma is hard to avoid in any business. Charge too little and you leave money on the table and lock yourselves into budget provider market perceptions. Charge too much and you fail to attract new customers and burn loyal customer relationships you spent years nurturing.

How do you find that price-demand 'sweet spot' for your products which locates the happy medium between price, demand, revenue and profit?

To have any chance of achieving this you first need to understand some basic pricing concepts:

- Price Elasticity
- Price Sensitivity
- Price Differentials
- Price and Product Maturity
- Pricing Psychology

Price Elasticity

Price Elasticity is the term used to describe the relationship between price and demand for a product and its target customers.

In simple terms if you increase price you reduce demand - but by how much? While you are reducing demand you must not forget that you are also increasing price and as revenue is units sold times unit price you are *potentially* increasing revenues and profits. So a key question in any price increase scenario is what will be the net effect of the increased price and the reduced demand on product revenues and profits.

For example, if you increase price by 10% and this has the effect of reducing demand by only 5% then you will have a net increase in revenues of approximately 5%. If in this simple example you continue to operate at the same net margin (probably unlikely) then you will have increased your profits by the same percentage.

Why 'approximately' 5%? You can check it out with a simple concrete example:

Before Price Increase
Unit Price = £10
Units Sold = 1000
Revenue Sold = £10,000
Net Margin = 20%
Profit Earned = £2,000

After 10% Price Increase
Unit Price = £11 (£10 + 10%)
Units Sold = 950 (1000 − 5%)
Revenue Sold = £10,450 (a 4.5% increase)
Net Margin = 20% (for example)
Profit Earned = £2,090 (4.5% increase)

However, I just plucked the "10% price increase equals 5% demand increase" out of thin air. To find the actual equation you would need to conduct market experiments and/or market research. If you do this for multiple price changes then you have created your 'Price Elasticity Curve' for the product. This curve will predict the impact of any price increase on demand for a particular product and set of customers.

It is important to note that no matter how precise and detailed your price elasticity curve is – it is still only a prediction! There is no guarantee that your product's price elasticity will behave exactly this way. For example, your market sample might have been too small or skewed with an imbalance of customers. Alternatively, when you did your market experiment there might have been other factors present in your market (such as different competitor pricing) which are not present now.

A simplified Price Elasticity Curve is shown overleaf to illustrate 3 important concepts:

The Cliff
This is the price increase point beyond which demand
drops rapidly (as in falls off a cliff). Beyond the cliff your
product is no longer a viable proposition for most of your
customers.

The Wall
This is the price decrease point below which demand no
longer increases (hits the wall). In effect you are wasting
your money reducing your price any further.

The Zone of Indifference
On this part of the curve changing price has little impact
on demand. In other words, demand is indifferent to price
changes between the price points in this zone.

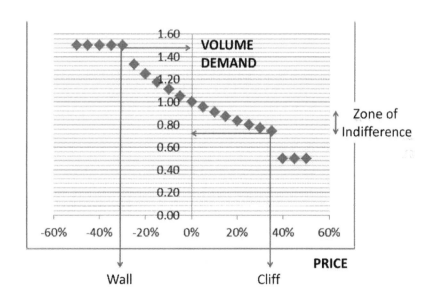

This example curve tells us that if the price is increased by 20% (x-axis) the demand drops to 80% of its level when the price was zero. Conversely if the price is decreased by 20% the demand rises by 20%. So this example is a simple 'symmetrical' price elasticity curve which would not necessarily be exactly the case in real life.

Your price 'Sweet-Spot' for this product is that point, somewhere above the Wall and below the Cliff, which leads to the optimum revenue/profits. It is important that this Sweet-Spot is also sustainable and will not lead to customer attrition over time as customers gradually become unhappy with, begin to resent and ultimately reject your product-price proposition.

Price Sensitivity

The Price Elasticity Curve helps you understand the 'Price Sensitivity' of a product.

For products with 'low price sensitivity' you can change the price and the demand may not change much. An example of low price sensitivity is if you decide to treat yourself to a cup of coffee in the lobby of a 5-star hotel. You already know that in Starbucks it would cost $2 for an expresso. As you take in the opulence of the luxury hotel you silently decide that you hope the bill will not be more than $5 but even if it is $10 you will pay it, especially if you have a guest!

Low price sensitivity is usually associated with premium, luxury or unique/novel products. However, it can also apply where there is a scarcity – if it's the last ticket for the big game and you really want to go then you are unlikely to quibble about the price.

For products with 'high price sensitivity' however a change in price may have a large impact on demand. Let's take the coffee example again. If instead of visiting the luxury hotel you decide to try out the mobile coffee cart at the train station for your regular morning espresso. Now your mental process is a bit different. You hope it will cost you less than $2 but you are prepared to pay $3 without an argument. However, if it is $2.50 or more than you are not going back! On the other hand, if it is good espresso (more later on the chapter on the relationship between price and quality) and the price is $1 or less then you might switch permanently.

In this example the coffee purchase is now highly price-sensitive. If the price goes up your demand will drop rapidly and if the price drops your demand will increase.

Usually high price sensitivity is associated with commodity or high competition products. Examples include home internet services, mobile phone subscriptions, basic staples such as milk and bread, and popular consumer services and products.

In both these examples the price sensitivity is 'symmetric' – i.e. the demand falls or rises in much the same way for both price increases and price decreases. This does not have to be the case – a product could have high sensitivity to price increases but low sensitivity to price decreases. In other words, if you put the price up then you lose customers but if you put the price down you don't win more customers. Similarly, a product or service could have low sensitivity to price increases but high sensitivity to price decreases. In other words, if you put the price up customers still buy but if you put the price down you win more customers.

Price Differentials

If you have been closely following the discussion on pricing, you might have noticed that to say that your product price directly impacts demand is in fact a simplification. It would be absolutely correct if yours was the only product of its kind in the market. However, most products have competition with their market and within their niche.

In this situation demand depends not so much on your absolute product price but the 'differential' between your price and your competitors' prices.

If you are a 'Premium' or 'Luxury' brand this means that customers expect there to be a positive differential between your product and other comparable products. On the other hand, if you are a 'Budget', 'Economy' or 'Commodity' customers expect you to have a negative differential, or not more than parity between yourself and other brands.

The previous discussion on Price Elasticity now applies in exactly the same way to *'Price Differential Elasticity'*. If you are a premium brand, then you should be very cautious about getting involved in a price (differential) war as your prospective customers are insensitive to price reductions so you will be leaving money on the table. You may also damage your premium position and confuse consumers as to the 'value gap' between your brand and budget brands.

On the other hand, if you are a budget brand you must be very careful about price differential increases as your target customers are very sensitive to price increases.... unless you can justify them in the eyes of the customer.

Breaking the rules of Price Demand

There is a fascinating online article [1] by *Fred Wilson* with comments by *Sean Black* which identifies 2 situations where price goes up but demand does <u>not</u> go down:

'There are two types of good for which peoples' purchase goes up as the price goes up, violating the law of demand: Giffen goods and Veblen goods. With a Giffen good, consumers keep buying as the prices go up because there really isn't a good substitute and these goods are a basic necessity. The common example is staple foods like rice.

With Veblen goods on the other hand, greater price means greater status. Veblen goods usually include luxury goods like wine, luxury cars, and designer goods.

The more expensive it is, the fewer people who can own it, the more it makes a statement for those that can'.

Price Support

This brings us to the important subject of 'Price Support'. Every time we spend money we have an expectation of an exchange of value being received. If I have been paying $2 for a cup of coffee and I am suddenly asked to pay $3 then my automatic thought process will be "what am I getting for my extra $1"?

If I cannot find a satisfactory explanation for this, then I will actively look for alternatives to restore the status quo and the $1 price increase will not be sustainable.

So the general rule in the market is that the consumer needs to be given a value proposition which makes the price increase palatable. The main tools for achieving this value proposition are quality, innovation, packing and marketing. The best scenario is when we invest in at least one of the first 3 (quality, innovation, packing) and then use marketing to tell the consumers about it!

Some companies will try to just use marketing to put a perceived extra value on the product but this can backfire. Other companies make the mistake of improving the product but forgetting to tell the consumer about it (expecting it to be obvious to them) and this seldom succeeds either. The general rule is that price increases need to be supported by both a value improvement and marketing. Just doing one is rarely enough and doing neither when you increase price is a recipe for failure.

If you would like to explore price support in more detail you might find the concept of the *Value Equivalence Line* that allows you to examine the difference between *Customer Value* and *Customer Perceived Value* and is explained very nicely in an article in the McKinsey Quarterly [2].

Price and Product Maturity

Another important pricing topic is the relationship between price and product maturity. Product/Pricing strategists tell us we should resist discounting price if a product is a market leader and is still in its prime.

However, if a product is not (or no longer seen as) a market leader then it may make sense to offer discounts to boost sales. However, this needs to be done in a sensitive way through special offers or retailer cash-back schemes, otherwise this can send the wrong message to the market. Just think of the shops which have permanent 50% sales signs up.

What do you consider the Retail Prices to actually be - the 100% price or the 50% discounted price?

Product Maturity Discounting is prevalent in industries such as automotive and mobile phones. It is usually achieved through dealer discounts and generous trade-in schemes which are actually paid for by the manufacturers (and known as "Dealer/Distributor Support" schemes).

Pricing Psychology

The whole psychology of pricing is a major topic in itself and well worth studying further. Here, by way of introduction, I will just highlight a couple of points.

Once we increase or reduce a price (or differential) then this will have an initial impact on demand according to the price elasticity of the product. However, if we keep the price at this level for an extended period then the new price or differential will become the new price-demand base point and demand will return towards the same level it was before we adjusted price.

I call this *Price-Demand Memory* and it is a good thing for premium products (price increasers) and a bad thing for budget brands (price reducers). In the latter case you may get an initial demand boost when you decrease your price but this can turn out just to be a blip and you then are stuck with lower revenues (same units sold but at a lower price).

This can also apply where you offer a free service ('freemium' model) for a limited period in the hope that you will convert a sufficient number of subscribers to a paid model by the end of the trial period. The problem is that conversion rates in this scenario are very low for the very reason that *Price-Demand Memory* can lock the service in the subscriber's minds as a zero price value proposition.

Proponents of the freemium model have an interesting dilemma as subscribers reach the end of the free period. Do they switch them off or do they let them continue but on a lower functionality free subscription? In the first option they force subscribers to either upgrade or quit and in the second option they accept a lower rate of immediate upgrades in the hope of more upgrades in the long run.

Another important area is where we are given a choice between different product/pricing offers. Dan Ariely in his excellent book 'Predictably Irrational' [3] explores how price strategists use behavioral economics [4] to encourage us to make choices which are best for the seller rather than the customer. Dan suggests humans 'don't have an internal value meter that tells us how much things are worth. Rather, we focus on the *relative advantage* of one thing over another, and estimate value accordingly'.

We can be cunningly manipulated where we are presented with various pricing choices. One common technique, known as *Decoy Pricing*, illustrated in the book with different subscription options for 'The Economist', is to encourage us to go for the most expensive option by making the most rational option (the cheapest one) seem very bad value compared with it.

Tom Sirett, from Twinings Ovaltine, who provided some excellent insights which improved this chapter, believes that the emerging discipline of Pricing Psychology is rapidly becoming more important than the classical economics school of pricing. For further reading in this fascinating area it is worth reading Daniel Kahneman's work on cognitive biases on pricing [5].

SELF-REFLECTION EXERCISE

1. *How/where does the 'Pricing Dilemma' manifest itself most strongly in your organization or team?*

2. *Can you identify some recent examples where difficult choices had to be made around Pricing?*

3. *Can you select one of these examples and use the Creative Dilemma Resolution process to brainstorm an alternative response?*

FURTHER READING on Pricing

1. *Setting value, not price*, McKinsey Quarterly, 1997 http://www.mckinsey.com/insights/marketing_sales/setting_value_not_price
2. *Price: Why Lower Isn't Always Better*, Fred Wilson, 2010, http://avc.com/2010/04/price-why-lower-isnt-always-better/
3. *Predictably Irrational: The Hidden Forces That Shape Our Decisions*, Dan Ariely, HarperCollins, 2008
4. *Behavioral Economics* http://www.mindbites.com/lesson/7093-behavioral-economics
5. *Thinking Fast and Slow*, Daniel Kahneman , Penguin 2012

Dilemma#4: Mix

The Mix Dilemma is fundamentally about how we mix (i.e. optimize) the different options available to us in terms of products, markets and other factors (such as supply, geography and currency) to produce the best business results at the lowest business risk.

The whole **business risk** issue merits exploring further with a question for you?

Do you see any problem with an enterprise producing a fantastic set of business results by taking huge risks?

Your initial response might be that there would be no problem whatsoever. But if you think about it more you might instead conclude that if a business does this *habitual risk gambling* year on year then one year the risks may not come off and then it's business results could be a total disaster.

In terms of Corporate Governance, investors generally prefer enterprises which deliver consistent year-on-year profits above enterprises who deliver an alternating mix of brilliant and terrible business results.

To achieve the former rather than the latter, businesses can adopt a portfolio approach to mixing their products, markets and operational risks.

Product Mix

One very common Mix dilemma is how to decide which of your products you should put the biggest sales and marketing resources into at any given time.

For example, let's imagine you are a provider of Real-Time Entertainment and you have 3 main on-demand products:

- Live Music
- Movies
- Sporting Events

Imagine the first and simplest scenario where you must mix your products to best react to weather. If you get a forecast of extremely inclement weather, then you might consider that this should result in a higher level of cancellations of Music and Sporting events than is normally the case.

What might you do to optimize your business results in the next period?

One obvious thing you might consider is putting extra resources into Movies at the expense of your other products. You might invest the bulk of your marketing budget here and go out of your way to maximize the range of movies available.

Let's imagine an alternative scenario with blistering hot weather predicted. How might this affect the demand for your different products? Where should you invest in marketing and supply in this instance?

Moving beyond weather into other scenarios – what should you do if there is a major international soccer competition coming up mid-year? Should you invest in Sporting Events? Alternatively, you might consider that your marketing has already been largely done for you and you should instead focus on the percentage of your audience who will be desperately looking for some alternatives to watching soccer!

Another classic dilemma here is what do you do when customer preferences indicate that one of your products has gone out of favor? You have two options – you can adjust your mix to accommodate customer preferences or you can invest your sales and marketing efforts in attempting to change them.

Which one would be best?

The generally accepted market wisdom is that unless you are the market leader in terms of company and product market share then you should generally try and accommodate customer preferences rather than trying to change them.

If you talk to venture capitalists, they may tell you that there are certain phrases which they do not want to hear when they are listening to a pitch from a company seeking investment funding. One of these phrases is "we will change customer behavior" as human nature and our resistance to change can make this is incredibly difficult to achieve.

In fact, research [1] shows that to make you or I change from a current product our service to a new one it must be *significantly better* and not just a bit better or we will stick with the status quo.

'You need to make sure your product is 10x better than that of your competitors.'

Bill Gross, Internet Pioneer

Market Mix

If you are trading internationally then you may have a choice of different geographic markets you can operate in. In generally markets can be categorized using 2 primary variables – market size and market growth.

You will be very fortunate if you can find markets for your products which are all large market size <u>and</u> high market growth. Most target markets are either Large/Low Growth, Small/High Growth or Medium Size/Medium Growth. (The other combination Small/ Low Growth markets are generally not attractive business expansion propositions).

Large/Low Growth and Medium/Medium markets are associated with mature markets which also have high levels of competition and regulation. Small/High Growth Markets, which are usually referred to as 'emerging markets', tend to be much smaller but with much lower levels of competition and regulation.

Along the same lines as the discussion of Product Contribution in our chapter on Products we can also ask ourselves what is the Market Contribution from each potential market?

The obvious rationale for being in Large/Low Growth and Medium/Medium markets is that these will provide the lion's share of the revenue for the whole enterprise. There is also a less obvious but equally important reason according to Professor Michael Porter, in his seminal work 'On Competition' [2]. Porter developed a '5-forces' framework for establishing the level of competition within any market:

1. Threat of new entrants
2. Threat of substitute products or services
3. Bargaining power of customers
4. Bargaining power of suppliers
5. Intensity of competitive rivalry

Large/Low Growth and Medium/Medium markets can give you access to the most competitive markets. One important aspect of these markets is that they are populated with the most demanding customers. If you build your business around satisfying these customers, then the argument goes you will also be able to satisfy the less demanding ones. Conversely if you build your business around satisfying the "easy" customers then you will not be forced to be as competitive as you could be.

In addition, such markets are difficult for other new entrants to enter so if you can successfully enter then you can establish have a strong position of 'defendable advantage' where the cost of entry to new competitors is simply too high.

Small/High Growth Markets are the emerging Stars which you hope may become your Cash Cows in the future according to the Boston Matrix Analysis (See under Product Chapter). They may not initially be high revenue contributors but because there are lower levels of competition then the profit levels can be very good. Also as they often have lower levels of regulation you have more freedom to experiment with new products and new channel approaches.

Market/Product Mix

Once you understand your Products and your Markets you are in a strong position to develop a strong portfolio position of products and markets.

You can then create a 3x3 grid with Products on one axis with 3 choices (Cash Cows, Stars and Question Marks) and Markets on the other axis with 3 choices (Mature, In Between and Emerging).

The next stage is to overlay on top of this all your product-in-market combinations to see if you are missing any obvious opportunities. Even more importantly you can also 'what-if' the effect of different market scenarios such as very high growth in an emerging market or negative growth in an established market.

There are a number of other Mix dilemmas including:

Supply Mix

How reliant are you on a single supplier and what would happen if this supplier got into difficulties? A real dilemma here is whether to have a single supplier and really work to develop them but with the risks of perhaps them not being as competitive as they could be on costs.

Alternatively, a split supplier policy allows for less supplier development but gives the opportunity of competitive procurement and reduces the risk of single supply problems.

Geography Mix

This is about balancing different geographies for supply and manufacturing to mitigate against the risk of a natural disaster or other event disrupting manufacturing or supply.

A real example of this is the devastating floods in Thailand which caused a 28 % quarter-on-quarter drop in laptop hard disk drive production in 2012 due to a number of the main supplier factories being closely located [3].

Currency Mix

For most global enterprises manufacturing, supply and
sales will span more than one currency. This creates a
currency risk which also needs to be managed.

An example would a US-based manufacturer with a large
market in China and suppliers in Eastern Europe. They
could be earning revenues in Chinese Yuan, incurring
manufacturing costs in US Dollars and buying components
and raw materials in Euros. So for example, if the Yuan or
the Euro depreciates against the US Dollar then the
revenues earned will be reduced but the costs incurred will
remain the same thus reducing profits.

Typically, such risks are managed through a treasury
function which attempt to 'hedge' the risks. An additional
more strategic and long-term approach to address this risk
is to spread manufacturing and major suppliers globally so
that the enterprises largest biggest sales market are
supplied locally. This is more difficult when a major
market is also a high cost market and can also increase
manufacturing management complexity.

We will discuss the vital topic of Risk Management more in
the (Organizational) Health Dilemma Chapter.

SELF-REFLECTION EXERCISE

1. *How/where does the 'Mix Dilemma' manifest itself most strongly in your organization or team?*

2. *Can you identify some recent examples where difficult choices had to be made around Mix?*

3. *Can you select one of these examples and use the Creative Dilemma Resolution process to brainstorm an alternative response?*

FURTHER READING on Mix

1. 'Why Habits Are Hard to Change (And Printers Hard to Buy)', Psychology Today Magazine, 2010
2. *The Competitive Strategy: Techniques for Analyzing Industries and Competitors*, Michael Porter, Free Press, 2004
3. 'Thai Floods Hit Q4 Hard Drive Production, Says Research Firm', PC World Magazine, 2011

Dilemma#5: Supply & Demand

The Supply & Demand Dilemma is primarily about how we strike a balance between having too much supply of our product (or its components) and having too little to satisfy our customer's demand and how we achieve this in the most profitable manner.

Balancing Supply and Demand is one of the most common and challenging business dilemmas. If you have an over-supply situation you can end up with too much product or stock which might be impossible to sell or only sellable through deep discounts. If you have an under-supply situation then you may disappoint customers, some of whom may turn to your competitors for their future requirements.

There are two main functions of an enterprise where Supply and Demand problems most often show up if communications with Sales are poor – Manufacturing and Procurement. I will look at each of these in turn.

Push vs. Pull

There are two typical approaches to balancing supply and demand in manufacturing – Push and Pull.

'Push' is the most traditional approach which works by generating sales forecasts which then become the basis for manufacturing forecasts. A key principle of 'Push' is to keep the manufacturing lines running wherever possible. The main issue with this approach is that if the sales forecasts are wrong, usually on the over-optimistic side, then you can quickly end up in an over-supply scenario. 'Push' is supported by sophisticated systems for Manufacturing Resource Planning and Enterprise Resource Planning (MRP and ERP) [1].

'Pull' is the alternative approach and is a central principle of Lean or Just-in-Time-Manufacturing [2]. The idea behind 'Pull' is that any product manufactured in advance of a committed customer order should be considered as waste. Therefore, you should not drive your manufacturing from (uncertain) Sales forecasts but rather from (certain) Customer Orders.

The original seven wastes of Lean [3] are:

1. *Transport* (moving products that are not actually required to perform the processing)
2. *Inventory* (all components, work in process, and finished product not being processed)
3. *Motion* (people or equipment moving or walking more than is required to perform the processing)
4. *Waiting* (waiting for the next production step, interruptions of production during shift change)
5. *Overproduction* (production ahead of demand)
6. *Over Processing* (resulting from poor tool or product design creating activity)
7. *Defects* (the effort involved in inspecting for and fixing defects)

'Overproduction' (point 5 on the above list) however is probably where the Pull philosophy differs most from Push.

Both Push and Pull approaches have their advocates. High volume, standard, short turnaround product businesses find Pull works best for them. However, businesses which undertake work which is more project than product such as heavy engineering tend to find that Push is more practical. There are also companies who take a hybrid approach using Pull for their high volume/product orders and Push for the low volume/project orders.

The Organizational Chasm: Sales vs. Manufacturing

Whether you are a supporter of Pull or Push one of the main challenges is the quality of communications between Sales and Manufacturing. (I use the term 'Manufacturing' in the broadest sense to include people resourcing if the business is providing a service rather than a product).

Sales will always be concerned with maximizing demand through activities such as marketing, advertising, price promotion and other campaigns.

Manufacturing will always be concerned with optimizing the use of production resources by keeping production at efficient levels. What this actually means in practice depends on whether they are operating a Push or Pull philosophy. Far-sighted manufacturing may also be attempting to manage additional virtual capacity which can be switched-on or bought-in at relatively short notice.

Good communications between Sales and Manufacturing are vital. Problems start when Sales make optimistic forecasts without thinking of the manufacturing implications. Sales can also cause significant problems if they behave as if they believe manufacturing has unlimited capacity with a "If we sell it they will have to deliver it" approach!"

Manufacturing can also significantly contribute to the problem if they are regularly unable to meet customer demand yet fail to make any future provisions for fixing this problem.

Challenges in Procurement

Many businesses have to buy raw materials or components to include in their finished products. Procurement will naturally want to get the highest quality product at the lowest possible price and shortest lead time.

In response to demands for lower prices suppliers usually tie discounts to increased volumes. This can exacerbate the supply and demand dilemma if to secure the lowest possible supply costs you have bought the highest possible volume. This risks putting the business into an over-supply situation.

Alternatively, if you are mindful of this risk you might have bought much less (at a higher cost) and face the other risk of even higher costs if your customer demand is higher than forecast to avoid an under-supply scenario.

When you buy aggressively in terms of volume you are said to be going 'Long' on the item. Whereas if you buy cautiously in terms of volume you are said to be going 'Short' on the item.

Volatile Procurement Markets

The issue of going Long or Short can become particularly tricky when the price of the item you are buying fluctuates widely. An example of where this happens is when you are procuring commodities such as Wheat or Grain or Oil whose price is traded on international commodity exchanges. Such prices can fluctuate widely due to private speculators and the whims of national/international politics.

A very real example here is a major flour manufacturer who buys different grades of wheat to make their different types of flour. Such an operation will regularly find themselves in one of two dilemmas:

Wheat Price is Low and predicted to Rise:

In this case should they go 'long' at the risk of being over-stocked with wheat if customer orders don't come through? If they have read the market correctly, they will be able use all the extra 'cheap' wheat to satisfy customers and maximize profit margins. However, if, instead, they have misread the market they may find that they could have bought the extra needed wheat later and cheaper and still satisfied their customers at even better profit margins.

Wheat Price is High and Likely to Fall:

In this case should they go 'short' at the risk of being under-stocked with wheat if customer orders do come through. If they have read the market correctly, they will be able to pick up the extra wheat at a lower price but if they have misread the market they may have to buy the wheat at an even higher price to avoid letting down customers. In this scenario their profit margins could be destroyed.

Risk Management and Good Governance

A useful business principle which applies to all Supply and Demand dilemmas is that you should never 'bet your business' on a single judgement call such as reading the market well.

Your business must be able to survive and achieve minimum thresholds of performance even if you do make a bad judgement call. (For more on this see the Results dilemma chapter). Getting the judgement call right may lead to stellar profits but it will be unacceptable to your investors if getting it wrong leads to catastrophic losses.

You need to have a 'plan B' for what will happen when each big judgement call turns out to be a bad one. This requires clear 'Policies' set in advance such as "we will procure to always cover committed customer demand plus 50% of expected demand" We will discuss Risk Management in more detail in the (Organizational) Health Dilemma Chapter.

SELF-REFLECTION EXERCISE

1. *How/where does the 'Supply and Demand Dilemma' manifest itself most strongly in your organization or team?*

2. *Can you identify some recent examples where difficult choices had to be made around Supply and Demand?*

3. *Can you select one of these examples and use the Creative Dilemma Resolution process to brainstorm an alternative response?*

FURTHER READING on Supply & Demand

1. *Making MRP Work: A Practical Guide To Improve Your System's Performance*, Giles Johnston, 2013
2. *Lean Principles with Practice*, Fraser and Fraser, 2013
3. The 7 Wastes of Lean Manufacturing
    https://en.wikipedia.org/wiki/Lean_manufacturing

Dilemma#6: Planning

The Planning Dilemma is essentially about getting the right balance between developing comprehensive plans and mobilizing plans through conversations. It is also about how we avoid the artifacts of planning becoming ends in themselves.

NOTE: I was originally going to call this chapter the 'Strategy' dilemma but I decided that although strategy was a major part of the dilemma I needed a slightly broader term. So when I say Planning Dilemma here its really shorthand for Planning/Preparing our Position plus Planning/Preparing our Execution.

First we need to briefly review 4 of the main tools for planning, positioning and organizing:

- Competitive Advantage
- Strategy
- Tactics & Plans
- Values

I will then look at 3 very common dilemmas in planning.

Competitive Advantage

Competitive Advantage, simply put, is what your organization has or could have which your competition doesn't have or can't practically have in the future.

A Systematic Guide to Business Acumen and Leadership using Dilemmas

I start with Competitive Advantage because, as Jack Welch famously said, 'If you don't have a competitive advantage, don't compete.'

There are 3 really important things about Competitive Advantage. Firstly, it must be sustainable. If your competitors can quickly copy it then any advantage will be short-lived indeed. Sustainable competitive advantage creates 'barriers to entry' for potential competitors and can go well beyond simply your products and services to patents, licenses, contracts, market access, supply chains and exclusive relationships.

Secondly, competitive advantage must give you an advantage over the others or in the words of the British Army:

'If you find yourself in a fair fight, you didn't plan your mission properly.'

Thirdly, despite our desire to create sustainable competitive advantage, and no matter how hard we work to keep it, so ultimately all competitive advantages decay. Therefore, we need to keep inventing new competitive advantages. Arie de Geus [1], a leading thinker in this area takes this line of thought eloquently to its logical conclusion:

'The ability to learn faster than your competitors may be the only sustainable competitive advantage.'

So Competitive Advantage and Organizational Health are closely linked. (see chapter on Organizational Health Dilemma).

Strategy

If you can identify some actual or potential sources of competitive advantage, then you are then in a good position to devise a strategy.

There are a many different definitions of Strategy but one of the most useful is proposed by the authors of the book '*Playing to Win*' [2].

'Strategy is a coordinated and integrated set of 5 choices – a winning aspiration, where to play, how to win, core capabilities, and management systems.'

So strategy is a clear ambition, a field of play, competitive advantage, plus the necessary skills and systems to make it happen.

Another very useful way of thinking about strategy is that if done well it can take your Competitive Advantage, and using it, 'design the circumstances where your success becomes inevitable'. [3].

Another approach to Strategy which has become popular in the last 10 years is 'Blue Ocean Strategy' [4] which suggests that instead of trying to compete with the competition in existing market spaces companies should instead create 'uncontested market spaces' which are free of competition. Such spaces can be highly profitable and if developed cleverly and powerfully can create first mover advantage and significant barriers to entry for the competition.

One of the most useful tools in Blue Ocean Strategy is the 'strategy canvas' which is a simple line chart of the 5-10 key indicators in an uncontested market space. The strategy canvas plots how a blue ocean position needs to be radically different from that of the current/traditional competitors, over these key indicators, to establish a genuine uncontested market space.

One very important tool many companies use in developing strategy is the old-fashioned but highly effective SWOT analysis [5] where you look *internally* at your own Strengths and Weaknesses and *externally* to identify the Opportunities and Threats presented by your Target Markets.

The *Value Proposition* is another useful tool here and represents what new value the customer obtains from consuming or using your product or service.

Plans and Tactics

'Strategy without tactics is the slowest route to victory. Tactics without strategy is the noise before defeat.' (Sun Tzu)

Once you have a strategy you need to think about how you are going to achieve it, to what degree and in what timeframe. This will require detailed plans with clear milestones. You will also need a detailed set of Key Performance Indicators (KPIs) which cover not just the top-line business results required but also provide detailed tracking and early warning systems. Such a measurement system is discussed in the chapter on the Results Dilemma.

Finally, your plans must address what Roles and Accountabilities the key leaders in the organization will play in delivering the strategy. To deliver a strategy will need a strong network of commitments starting at the top of the organization and spreading to all layers of management. You can read more about the discipline of commitments in the chapter about the Agility Dilemma.

Values and Behaviors

Albert Einstein is credited with defining *insanity* as 'doing the same thing over and over again and expecting different results.'

If your strategy and plan can be achieved with no change whatsoever in the behaviors of you or your colleagues, then I would contend that you are either in denial or perhaps the strategy itself is lacking in ambition and scale. Either way you are unlikely to achieve great success. Somewhere along the line an organization needs to seriously explore the following kinds of question:

- What do we stand for?
- What do we want our customers to say about us?
- How are we going to treat our people?

- What will we NEVER do – even in a crisis?
- What will we ALWAYS do – even in a crisis?
- Where do we currently fall short of what we want to be?
- What are the stories and anecdotes which make us proud?
- What are the stories and anecdotes which make us ashamed?

The answers to these kinds of questions can help us define our 'core values' and 'core behaviors', to identify where we fall short and what we need to do to close the gap.

There seem to be 3 very common dilemmas in the broad planning area:

Written Word vs. Spoken Word

One dilemma that comes up over and over again concerns the communication process. In their ground-breaking book '*Computers and Cognition*' [6] the authors explore the ambiguity of language and show that almost any written statement is open to multiple interpretations.

There seems to be a natural bias to overly rely on written communications about strategy, plans, roles and goals. From my experience nobody should ever accept a serious goal without a real conversation of clarification with the person setting the goal!

As well as the ambiguities and deficiencies of the written word we also have the ambiguities and deficiencies of numbers. For example, consider the goal below:

Your goal is to achieve financial growth of at least 15% on last year's performance which was:

Sales: *$65.0 M*
Net Margin   *20%*
Net Profits   *$13.0 M*

Can you see any possible ambiguities in this goal?

For example, does the 15% also apply to the margin (making it 23% as opposed to 20%)? This would increase the profit target from $15M (20% of $75M) to $21M (23% of $75M). It could make a big difference to your bonus if you discovered halfway through the financial year that your profit target was $6M greater than you thought it was?

So is the goal to improve margin or to maintain margin? Again the ambiguities of language and intention can catch you out.

So we should always resist the temptation to accept a **naked written goal** without a real conversation no matter how clear it seems. We should ask questions like:
- Can you restate the goal verbally in another way?
- How will you judge if I have achieved the goal?
- Why are you asking <u>me</u> to do it?

- How might I achieve this goal and yet fail to satisfy you?
- Why do you want this goal achieved?

Change vs. Preservation

In one of my business simulation games we ask teams to devise their strategy for taking over the running of a very successful business unit. In almost all cases the teams fixate on what they need to <u>change</u> rather than what they need to <u>preserve</u>. [See Appendix A, finding 1, for more details].

It seems to be human nature and our natural insecurity that means when we take over something we feel we must quickly put our mark upon it. Inevitably this means changing things.

However, a mature leader will also spend time finding out what was good about the current situation, what should be preserved, what needs to be given credit for and what must NOT be allowed be lost.

Strategy vs. Action

One of the most common things I encounter in business simulations is teams who define a good clear strategy or set of values which tick all the boxes and then totally ignore it in all their decisions. See Appendix A, finding 5, for more details].

For example, we might state that an important team value is that 'every voice will be heard' but when the team gets put under pressure then one or two members just rush through a hurried decision.

Similarly, a key element of our strategy might be for our organization to be a 'Product Leader' but under pressure we forget this and put all our energies and investment into satisfying customers with existing products.

Teams who align strategy with action <u>under pressure</u> are said to demonstrate 'coherence'. Such teams are more likely to avoid 'Mission Drift' where teams can flip from one crisis to the next without ever improving their overall situation.

SELF-REFLECTION EXERCISE

1. *How/where does the 'Planning Dilemma' manifest itself most strongly in your organization or team?*

2. *Can you identify some recent examples where difficult choices had to be made around Strategy, Plans, Roles or Values?*

3. *Can you select one of these examples and use the Creative Dilemma Resolution process to brainstorm an alternative response?*

FURTHER READING on Planning

1. *The Living Company*, Arie de Geus and Peter Senge, Harvard Business School Press, 1997
2. *Playing to Win: How Strategy Really Works*, Lafley and Martin, Harvard Business Review Press, 2013
3. Lane 4 Performance, http://www.lane4performance.com/
4. *Blue Ocean Strategy: How To Create Uncontested Market Space And Make The Competition Irrelevant*, Kim and Mauborgne, 2005
5. SWOT Analysis, https://en.wikipedia.org/wiki/SWOT_analysis
6. *Understanding Computers and Cognition*, Winograd and Flores, Addison Wesley, 1987

Dilemma#7: Results

The Results dilemma concerns how we design and effectively monitor a balanced set of measures which keep our 'eyes on the prize' while providing us with effective tracking and early warning systems.

Leading and Lagging Indicators

One of the main dilemmas business leaders encounter is which results they should 'steer' by in terms of seeing how things are going. There are two main challenges – delays and fixation.

Many results, typically financial, happen long after the activity which caused them has ceased. These are referred to as 'lagging' indicators and are *outcome* measures. They are an essential perspective on a business as ultimately profits are what the business is there to generate. However, because they are lagging indicators they are not effective early warning indicators because by the time you see them all the activities which could have influenced them are over. Example lagging Indicators include Sales, Revenue, Costs and Profits.

Other results, typically non-financial, happen much in advance of the lagging indicators. These are referred to as 'leading' indicators and are *activity* measures. They are also an essential perspective on a business as they provide excellent early warning systems and can allow you to conduct a *Root Cause Analysis* of problems. However, because they are leading indicators they are not effective outcome measures and never tell the ultimate story of how a business is doing in a way which would satisfy its investors. Example leading indicators include proposals made per month, exit rates of customers, customer satisfaction levels and employee retention levels.

If you take the analogy of an aircraft pilot - airspeed and estimated time of arrival are lagging indicators whereas engine temperatures, altitude and headings are leading indicators.

One of the most common causes of airplane crashes is called CFIT (controlled flight into terrain) which means that pilots have flown a perfectly good plane into a hillside or the ground. How could this happen?

One of the main reasons it could happen is that the pilots spot an issue, typically accompanied by a warning light, and *fixate* on this single issue at the expense of the other critical indicators such as airspeed and altitude.

Malcolm Gladwell discusses the cultural issues around this in his book '*Outliers*' [1]. He dedicates a whole chapter to the concept of 'Power Distance' which inhibits junior pilots from correcting the mistakes of senior pilots in some cultures – even if they are flying the plane into the ground.

So to successfully manage the results of a business you need to have a balance of leading and lagging indicators and to avoid fixation on any one or two indicators at the expense of the others.

Balanced Scorecard

The approach I have outlined here is known as the Balanced Scorecard [2] approach to managing business developed by Robert Kaplan and David Norton. It is regarded as one of the best approaches to developing and managing to strategy and has a strong set of empirical evidence of business success.

The 4 Perspectives of the Balanced Scorecard

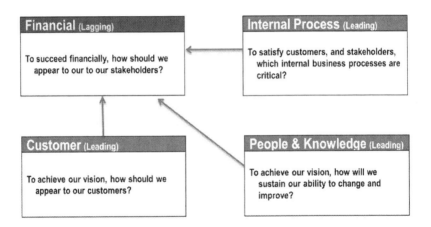

The Balanced Scorecard approach suggests that there are 4 key perspectives we should measure and track:

1. Financial
2. Customer
3. Process
4. Learning

The Financial perspective is generally a lagging or outcome class of measure which is driven by the other 3 perspectives which are generally leading indicators.

Balanced Scorecards are constructed by interviewing senior members of the organization to identify candidate indicators. To narrow these indicators down to a practical scorecard there a number of scorecard best practices such as:

- 1 or 2 lagging measures for every strategic objective
- If we have a choice of more than 1 measure, we should use the one that best tracks and communicates the intent
- Not more than 25 measures per scorecard

Cause and Effect

One of the most important aspects of developing a useful Balanced Scorecard is understanding and defining the relationships between the leading indicators and the lagging indicators. In Balanced Scorecard terminology these relationships are captured as Strategy Maps [2]. Elsewhere these are also known as Causal Maps, Root Cause Analysis and Cause and Effect Diagrams [3] because they help you differentiate between the visible effects and the often invisible root causes of a situation.

Such maps are immensely valuable because this is one of the biggest challenges you will ever face in business – am I fixing the cause of this problem or merely addressing one of its symptoms? If I fix the cause the problem should be solved but if I only fix a symptom the problem will probably keep coming back in different guises.

Let's look at an example Cause and Effect Diagram. Imagine an area of a business which is responsible for generating new sales. So we start on the right hand side of a blank page writing down SALES REVENUE. We then ask ourselves what causes this? We might say SALES ORDERS and AVERAGE ORDER VALUES. We write these to the left of SALES REVENUE. We then ask what causes these 2? We might decide that SALES ORDERS are the effects of SALES BIDS (or SALES PROPOSALS) and write it to the left. But what causes AVERAGE ORDER VALUE? That is a trickier point which we will return to soon!

If we continue we eventually construct a Cause and Effect diagram which might look something like the one overleaf:

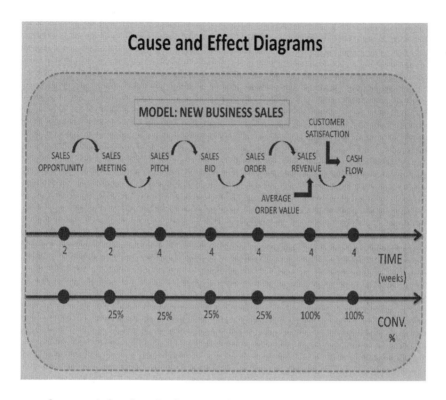

But how might that help us? There are a number of ways:

Firstly, we now know that if we have a problem with sales revenue (symptom) then the cause of this could be anything to the left of it on the diagram.

Secondly, if we add the timeline axis we can see that a problem in Sales Opportunities could take 18 weeks before it impacts sales revenue so sales revenue would not be a good early warning indicator of potential problems.

Thirdly, if we add the conversion axis we can see that to get 1 new sales order we would typically require 4 sales bids each of which would need 4 Sales Pitches each of which requiring 4 Sales Meetings and 4 Sales Opportunities. So to get 1 sale we would need $4*4*4*4 = 256$ Sales Opportunities. If our conversion rates are correct and we only have 25 Sales Opportunities in our pipeline, then this is a great early warning of another big problem which will show up 16 weeks later in Sales Revenue.

Cause and Effect Diagrams are very powerful tools. They also highlight flaws in our thinking about what the real drivers of business results are.

Also in terms of the Balanced Scorecard they link Financial results to the other perspectives of performance - Customers, Processes and Learning. In the example we indicated that receiving the actual customer payment will also be dependent on customer satisfaction (not happy = delay payment) which would be a key measure in the Customer Perspective aspect of the scorecard. In addition, our discussion about the causes of Average Order Values clearly connects to the Learning perspective if we discover that more experienced sales people have the highest order values and why that might be.

Uses of the Balanced Scorecard

Finally, there are two main uses of the Balanced Scorecard.

Firstly, it can be used for *Project Alignment* to check how much proposed (and even already underway) projects actually contribute to the strategic results required by the organization. Proponents of the Balanced Scorecard suggest that up to 25% of company projects are 'executive pet projects' which make little contribution to strategic goals and results. An effective Balanced Scorecard can be used to create compelling and rational arguments for killing these pet projects.

The second main use of the Balanced Scorecard is, of course, *Holistic Result Tracking*, where an organization can track all the many indicators needed for success including the leading indicators which will be vital in providing an effective early warning system when things are not going according to plan!

SELF-REFLECTION EXERCISE

1. *How/where does the 'Results Dilemma' manifest itself most strongly in your organization or team?*

2. *Can you identify some recent examples where difficult choices had to be made around which results to steer off?*

3. *Can you select one of these examples and use the Creative Dilemma Resolution process to brainstorm an alternative response?*

FURTHER READING on Results

1. *Outliers: The Story of Success*, Malcolm Gladwell, Penguin, 2009
2. *The Balanced Scorecard: Translating Strategy into Action*, Kaplan and Norton, Harvard Business Review Press, 1996
3. *Strategy Maps: Converting Intangible Assets into Tangible Outcomes*, Kaplan and Norton, Harvard Business Review Press, 2003
4. Root Cause Analysis, https://en.wikipedia.org/wiki/Root_cause_analysis

Dilemma#8: Health

The Health Dilemma is primarily about how we strike a balance between delivering the required results today whilst protecting and enhancing the ability of our organization to deliver the results it needs in the future.

Investing in TODAY'S business typically means investing money, resource and attention on activities which support winning, managing, and satisfying customers. In other words, *Customer Value Chain* activities. Wise investment here should generate income for the organization in the near-term.

Investing in TOMORROW'S business typically means investing in improving capabilities of the organization's people, processes, infrastructure, partnerships and technologies. In other words, *Organizational Health* Activities. Wise investment here should generate and protect income for the organization in the medium and long-term but not in the near-term.

If an organization invests too much in Customer Value Chain and not enough in Organizational Health, then it may achieve its short-term business results but at the expense of its future business results. It is a like a soccer team which has not replaced its best strikers but kept them playing past their prime. All of a sudden it will become no longer fit for purpose. Such organizations become burned out with terrible morale plus systems and processes which are not fit for purpose (which damages morale even further).

If an organization invests too much in Organizational
Heath and not enough in Customer Value Chain, then it
may be a very fit organization but one which is not meeting
its key operational targets. This is a like a soccer team who
are constantly introducing talented new and young players
from their academy but are not winning tough matches
any more.

Hence the Health Dilemma – what is the right balance of
investment between Customer Value Chain (securing
profits now) and Organizational Health (protecting future
profits)?

The figure below is a partial screenshot from the Xsim
Business Simulation Game (described in more detail in
Appendix A) which illustrates the different ways the
Health dilemma might manifest itself:

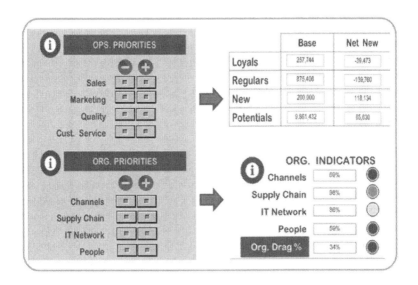

In this case the participants are allowed to choose 3 high priorities from a choice of 8. The top 4 choices concern the Customer Value Chain:

- Sales
- Marketing
- Quality
- Customer Service

Investment here immediately impacts the Customer Loyalty ladder (as described in the Customer Dilemma chapter) which are shown to the right.

The remaining 4 choices concern Organizational Health:

- Channels
- Supply Chain
- IT Network
- People

Investment here impacts the 'Maturities' of the 4 Health Factors which are shown to the right. However, the impact on these maturities is not immediate – for example, 'IT Network' may be a quicker fix than 'People'. Also the benefits of the investment may not be realized until the maturities reach certain minimum thresholds.

Each aspect of Organizational Health has a traffic light which reflects its individual health and contributes to the overall fitness of the organization. Where any one is deficient it also creates a 'drag factor' which applies to the

whole business. This brings us nicely to the concept of
Organizational Resilience.

Organizational Resilience.

'Resilience' can be defined as 'the capacity to recover
quickly from difficulties; demonstrating toughness.' *Diane
Coutu* has written an excellent paper on 'Personal
Resilience' [1] if you wish to explore this subject further.
However, for now, I am more interested in 'Organizational
Resilience'.

I would define Organizational Resilience as the ability of
an organization to absorb unexpected shocks without
destroying operational performance.

We can explain Organizational Resilience in a simple way
by considering 3 zones within which any of the different
capabilities of an enterprise such as People, IT and
Customer Services, must operate:

Capability Levels & Zones

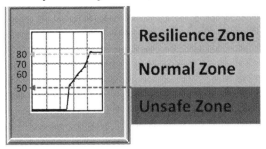

Normal Zone - If a capability is operating in the *Normal Zone* then it is at an acceptable/safe level and any capability improvement or decay will produce a commensurate change in business performance.

Resilience Zone – If a capability is operating in the *Resilience Zone* then it is at a higher level of capability than the business currently requires. This extra level of capability will <u>not</u> be delivering proportionately additional business performance but is there as an 'insurance policy' against potential future shocks.

Unsafe Zone – If a capability is operating in the *Unsafe Zone* then it is operating below the acceptable level and as a result is producing a disproportionately large impact on business performance.

Resilience is therefore expensive and like all insurance has to be invested in very selectively. The best way to do this is to conduct a risk assessment based on:

1. The most likely future shocks the business might encounter
2. The impact these shocks would have on the organization and its customers
3. The maturities of the supporting capabilities and that would need to be enhanced to absorb these shocks to an acceptable level

This approach allows the development of a practical business/customer-led organizational resilience plan. This can also be referred to as *Business Continuity Planning* [2].

SELF-REFLECTION EXERCISE

1. *How/where does the 'Organizational Health and Risk Dilemma' manifest itself most strongly in your organization or team?*

2. *Can you identify some recent examples where difficult choices had to be made around Organizational Health and Risk?*

3. *Can you select one of these examples and use the Creative Dilemma Resolution process to brainstorm an alternative response?*

FURTHER READING on Organizational Health

1. *How Resilience Works*, Diane Coutu, Harvard Business Review, 2002
https://hbr.org/2002/05/how-resilience-works

The Business Continuity Management Desk Reference, Jamie Watters, Leverage Publishing 2010

Dilemma#9: Agility

The Agility Dilemma is about our ability to respond effectively to and learn from all types of unexpected change both minor and major. It is also about how we design systems to warn of, build resilience to and respond to future shocks so that if they cannot be avoided or absorbed at least we can manage them with less pain.

Agility

Agility is an over-used word and in some respects has been somewhat hijacked by the IT profession under the term 'Agile' software development. This is a shame as Agility is in fact a very useful concept which simply means *the ability to handle unexpected change well.*

Change

There are some useful distinctions about the types of change which an organization and its people will encounter.

The first distinction about any change which we are subject to is explained concisely by the '3 Circles Model' which I first encountered in Stephen Covey's book 'Principle Centered Leadership' [1].

The 3 circles are *Control, Influence* and *Concern.*

The inner circle is the *Circle of Control* within which I can largely control anything which happens. For example, if I am a team leader then I can largely control what happens inside my team meetings. Unfortunately, this is the smallest circle.

The next circle is the *Circle of Influence*. I cannot control what happens here but I have some influence over it. For example, if I am a team member then I have some influence over what happens inside the team meetings.

The next circle is the *Circle of Concern* – I cannot control or even influence what happens here but what happens here concerns and impacts me. This is the largest circle.

Once a situation happens it is important to establish which of the 3 circles you/your organization are in with respect to it so that you avoid any wasted effort planning responses which will have no impact.

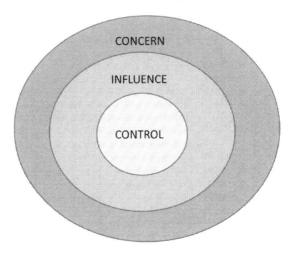

The second important distinction about change is *Planned vs. Unplanned* change where the former is initiated by the organization as part of a plan which requires 'Change Management'. My book on High Performing Teams and Change Management explores this topic in detail for readers who are interested [2].

In terms of *Unplanned Change* there are two different Severity Levels – 'Business Turbulence' and Urgent Situations/Crises. We will take look at each of these in this chapter.

Business Turbulence

I define 'Business Turbulence' as the normal ups and down of running a business. Examples include product recalls, poor customer satisfaction feedback, delays in the introduction of new IT systems, higher than average levels of staff attrition, poor weather impacting sales, market downturn, new government red-tape and competitor price rises.

The excellent book, *The Discipline of Market Leaders*[3], discusses how market leader choose one of 3 leadership positions in the market – Product Leadership, Customer Intimacy or Operational Excellence. The authors describe how different companies choose which of the 3 they wish to excel at. More importantly however for this discussion such companies do not neglect the other two positions but set <u>minimum thresholds</u> for them below which performance will not be allowed to slip.

This is a vital concept for successfully navigating business turbulence. You may not be able to maximize all your KPIs so who must decide two things:

1) Which Priority KPIs will be maximized?
2) What are the minimum thresholds for the other KPIs?

For example, in a market downturn, you might decide that profit targets must be hit but you will be prepared to accept lower growth than planned in market share provided it does not go backwards. This does not mean you have abandoned your market share targets, rather it means that when hard decisions have to be made then you already know and have agreed your priorities.

The two alternatives to this are trying to achieve everything during turbulence or making all hard decisions in the moment, on a case by case basis. Both approaches are flawed. For evidence of this check Appendix B (Top Performing Team Game Research – Finding 4).

Business 'Situations' (aka Crisis Management)

Unexpected Business Situations are major events (internal or external) that occur which could have a major impact on an organization. They can be Crises (-) or Major Opportunities (+). For example, a hostile take-over bid on one hand or the opportunity to acquire a major competitor on the other.

To deal with these situations you need to first have in place the same disciplines you use to deal with Business Turbulence.

However, these disciplines in themselves will not be enough– you will need 3 other disciplines:

1. Information Management
2. Commitment Management
3. Communications Management

Information Management

In a Crisis or a Major Opportunity, you may be dealing with an ever-changing situation and therefore you need to be organized in terms of managing the information and ensuring *the right people have the right information at the right time.* A temptation is to think that this is an IT problem. It is not – although when you have decided how you want to manage the information you may use IT but it should not be driven by IT.

It is relatively simple to design and operate an effective *Information Management Control Center* to allow you to access instantly and accurately the current status of your relevant KPIs plus any new updated/information, whether on paper, soft copy or verbal.

The diagram overleaf shows a simple 'Low-Tech' example of how you might structure such a Crisis Room or Information Management Control Center using simple In-trays, Information Registers and Decision log and a number of loose leaf folders.

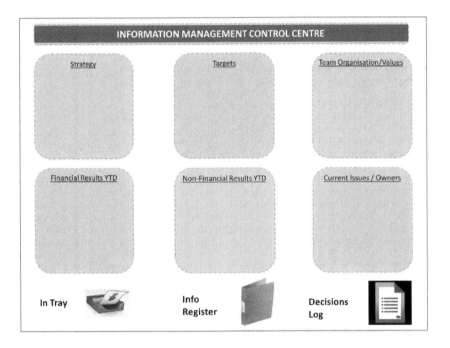

Commitment Management

It is even more important in a crisis that people do what they say they are going to do when they say they are going to do it. So you need a protocol for Managing Commitments which also allows for all the necessary communications, negotiations, and updates between the individuals involved.

Such a discipline is known as Commitment-based Management (CbM) [4]. The goal of CbM is to create a *network of commitments* in an organization.

Effective networks of commitment have certain key characteristics:

- *Conversational:* Co-invented in honest conversations between individuals acting as customers and performers
- *Authentic:* Freely made without duress and with the possibility of saying 'No'
- *Realistic:* Not beyond the reach of the performer
- *Challenging:* Not trivial - stretches the performer
- *Visible:* Not private, public to the individual's peers
- *Living:* Changing through negotiation as needed

Communications Management

The third key discipline in a crisis is to carefully manage what you say, when you say it and how you say it to all the people outside the Crisis Management team including other staff in the organization and very importantly external parties such as customers, the media and investors.

There is an excellent 3-page paper, How a Good Manager Reacts to a Crisis, in The Harvard Business Review [5] which addresses this point well and identifies 5 important points for leaders during a crisis:

1. Take time to figure things out first
2. Be prompt but not hasty
3. Manage Expectations
4. Demonstrate Control
5. Stay 'Loose' personally

Organizational Mindfulness

Now that the crisis is over what to you do? Do you just catch your breath and go back to 'business as usual' or do you try to take some learning from the crisis so it is less likely to be as impactful the next time? In other words, can you develop Organizational Mindfulness from it?

In today's busy, time-poor, always-on world Personal Mindfulness has become a very popular topic.

'Mindfulness' can be defined as 'the practice of maintaining a non-judgmental state of heightened awareness of one's thoughts, emotions, or experiences on a moment-to-moment basis.'

If you can make 'risk scanning' part of your day to day business life rather than just a 'ticking-the-boxes' kind of concern, then you can begin to develop 'Organizational Mindfulness.'

In the book '*Managing the Unexpected*' [6] the story is told of how Winston Churchill, the famous British Prime Minister during WWII, was suddenly faced with the horrendous discovery that Singapore was not secure as previously thought but, in fact, highly vulnerable to a Japanese invasion.

As a result of this shock, which could have changed the whole balance of the war, Churchill is credited with developing 4 questions which he would then always ask

when faced with such an unexpected situation in the
future:

1.   *Why didn't I know?*
2.   *Why didn't my advisors know?*
3.   *Why wasn't I told?*
4.   *Why didn't I ask?*

If, as a leader, you and your colleagues make it a habit to
constantly ask Churchill's 4 questions you will learn from
situations and become better at avoiding and mitigating
them in the future.

One of the most famous corporate manslaughter cases,
which came to trial during the late 1980s in the United
Kingdom, was when the Herald of Free Enterprise - a car
ferry - capsized in 1987 off the Belgian coast. A total of 193
lives were lost after the bow doors of the ferry failed to
close and the car deck was flooded.

An inquest jury returned verdicts of unlawful killing in 187
cases. However, the corporate manslaughter case failed
because the various acts of negligence could not be
attributed to any individual who was a "controlling mind".
[7]

Below is the relevant policy that the ship was subject to
concerning preparation for sea [8].

*'Heads of Departments are to report to the Master
immediately if they are aware of any deficiency which is
likely to cause their departments to be unready for sea in*

any respect at the due sailing time. In the absence of any such report the Master will assume, at the due sailing time, that the vessel is ready for sea in all respects.'
If you study this policy, you will notice that the management philosophy is "if no-one says anything is wrong then we assume that everything is OK."

This is the polar opposite mind-set to Organizational Mindfulness and was exposed as being a major contributing factor to the disaster when the ship sailed without the bow doors being properly secured.

However, if you take a minute to apply Churchill's 4 questions to the policy then its shortcomings become crystal clear. Question 4 in particular, 'Why didn't I ask?' puts leadership mindfulness center stage and could have made all the difference to the ship.

SELF-REFLECTION EXERCISE

1. *How/where does the 'Agility / Change Dilemma'
    manifest itself most strongly in your organization
    or team?*
2. *Can you identify some recent examples where
    difficult choices had to be made around Agility or
    Unexpected Change or Major Shocks?*
3. *Can you select one of these examples and use the
    Creative Dilemma Resolution process to
    brainstorm an alternative response?*

FURTHER READING on Agility

1. *Principle-Centered Leadership*, Stephen Covey, Rosetta Books, 2009
2. *A Systematic Guide to High Performing Teams* (HPTs), Ken Thompson, December 2015
3. *The Discipline of Market Leaders*, Treacy and Wiersema, Perseus Books 1996
4. *Promise-Based Management - The Essence of Execution*, Donald Sull and Charles Spinosa Harvard Business Review, 2007
5. *How a Good Manager Reacts to a Crisis*, John Baldoni, Harvard Business Review, 2001
6. *Managing The Unexpected*, Weik & Sutcliffe, Josssey Bass, 2001
7. History of corporate manslaughter: five key cases, The Telegraph Newspaper, 2011 http://www.telegraph.co.uk/finance/yourbusiness/8330905/History-of-corporate-manslaughter-five-key-cases.html
8. Standing Order 01.09 Ready for Sea, Herald of Free Enterprise, 1987

Dilemma#10: Team

The Team dilemma is how we balance the tensions of being an effective, autonomous, and motivating leader with being a supportive and loyal member of a senior team.

The Team dilemma is essentially a 'Me vs. We' conundrum. It encompasses all the tensions individuals face in leading teams at the same time as being members of other teams in which they are not the leader.

The 3 main areas of the Team dilemma are:

- Conflicting Styles
- Decisions and Decision-Making
- Coordination

Conflicting Styles

A wise person once said if you find the perfect team don't join it as you will spoil it. You can't be in an organization without being in a team and colleagues will annoy, exasperate and frustrate you. Whether we like it or not we have exactly the same effect on our colleagues.

What are the most common areas for friction around colleagues' personalities, behaviors and styles? One way to look at this is through personality tests. There are many different types of test, each of which use a different lens to look at people. One of the most popular is the *Myers*

Briggs Type Indicator (MBTI) [1] which categorizes individuals across 4 preferences:

1. Our favourite World
Are we Extraverts (E) or Introverts (I)?

Do we prefer the outer world or our own inner world?

2. How we handle Information
Are we Sensing (S) or are we Intuitive (N)?

'Sensors' prefer to focus only on the raw information whereas 'Intuitives' prefer to interpret information and add their own meaning?

3. How we make Decisions
Are we Thinking (T) or Feeling (F)?

'Thinkers' prefer to look at logic and consistency whereas 'Feelers' prefer to look more at the people and any special circumstances?

4. How to we like to Resolve things
Are we Judging (J) or Perceiving (P)?

'Judgers' prefer to get things decided whereas 'Perceivers' prefer to stay open and receptive to new information and options?

In MBTI an individual is classified according to the 4 preferences, which creates 16 different possibilities. For example, an 'ENTJ' prefers the outer world, likes the big picture, is very logical about decisions and likes to get things resolved quickly.

On the other hand, an 'ISFP' is the polar opposite of an ENTJ, preferring their inner world and the details of a situation. They also prefer to be more intuitive about decisions and don't need to decide so quickly. It is easy to see the tensions which an ENTJ might have working closely in a team with an ISFP.

Just to be clear I am NOT putting forward MBTI as a recommended approach in your organization. Like all tests MBTI has a number of shortcomings which are well documented [2]. However, I AM suggesting it can provide a useful way to see obvious areas of potential conflict between team members.

So to be more effective in dealing with team members it is helpful if we can develop an awareness of each other's styles and preferences. We don't have to do personality tests – we can simply talk with each other about would what we prefer in key areas such as:

- Listening vs. Talking
- Disclosing vs. Not Disclosing 'personal things'
- Information – do we prefer more or less?
- Thinking Time – do we prefer like to get information in advance of discussing?

Decisions and decision-making

Decisions and decision-making are two areas in themselves that can cause a huge amount of conflict between individuals in teams.

In terms of the *actual decisions* made it won't be long before we find ourselves holding the opposite position from some of our team members on a particular decision. If we feel strongly about it, we can try and win our colleagues round but this won't always succeed. Even if we do succeed in winning them round we may have alienated or bullied them in the process. So a frequent dilemma is whether any particular team decision is worth taking an individual stand over?

The next dilemma is where we have not been able to win our colleagues round (or decided not to try!) We can find ourselves in a team who have made a decision we don't agree with. This brings us to 'collective responsibility' or 'cabinet responsibility' as it is referred to in government.

We have to decide can we live with and actively support a decision which we don't agree with. Hopefully we can do this in most cases but if we can't we need to decide the best way to handle it. Ways NOT to handle it include keeping trying to re-run the team arguments to change the decision back or telling colleagues outside the team that the team has made a big mistake but you have to go along with it!

The second area for conflict is HOW the decisions are actually reached in the first place.

In the excellent book, *"Why Teams Don't Work"* [3], the authors identify 7 key decision making styles for teams. If a team is planning to make a major decision, it should, wherever possible, discuss and agree on how the decision will be reached (e.g. using one of these 7 styles) <u>before</u> the actual decision-making discussions start.

At the meeting, the team leader should introduce the decision which needs to be made and then propose the decision making style which is then discussed and agreed:

1.   Consensus
2.   Majority Rule
3.   Minority Rule
4.   Averaging
5.   Expert
6.   Authority Rule without Discussion
7.   Authority Rule with Discussion

In my book *'A Systematic Guide to High Performing Teams'* [4] I discuss decision-making and the other key topic of effective team meetings in much more detail for the reader who is interested in finding out more.

Coordination

The third dilemma for an individual in a team is how they handle the need to receive and give help and feedback. We all know people who function at various extremes. There are the 'lone rangers' who can delegate nothing or ever ask for help. There are the 'micro-managers' who try to do their colleagues jobs as well as their own. There are also the 'Teflons which nothing ever sticks to. 'Teflons' somehow seem to manage to avoid picking up any direct commitments or responsibilities whatever themselves.

What is really going on with these behavioral stereotypes?

If you look below the surface you will see that there are a couple of important values conversations which need to be had around Trust, Respect, and Commitment:

- Will I trust you with my reputation?
- Will I respect your reputation?
- Am I willing to make commitments to you?
- Will I trust the commitments you make to me?

If you see these stereotypes of bad co-ordination in your team it is often a warning that you need to revisit your team values (refer to the chapter on the Planning Dilemma) and/or your commitment management processes (refer to the chapter on the Agility Dilemma).

SELF-REFLECTION EXERCISE

1. *How/where does the 'Team Dilemma' manifest itself most strongly in your organization or team?*

2. *Can you identify some recent examples where difficult choices had to be made around Team?*

3. *Can you select one of these examples and use the Creative Dilemma Resolution process to brainstorm an alternative response?*

FURTHER READING on Team

1. The Myers Briggs Foundation, http://www.myersbriggs.org/my-mbti-personality-type/mbti-basics/
2. *The Myth of Personality Types: Exposing Pop Psychology's Biggest Scam*, Chance Ableson, Re Wired Books, 2016
3. *Why Teams Don't Work*: Robbins, Harvey, and Michael Finley, January 2000
4. *A Systematic Guide to High Performing Teams* (HPTs), Ken Thompson, December 2015

A Systematic Guide to Business Acumen
and Leadership using Dilemmas

Other Books by the Author

BIOTEAMS: High performance teams and virtual groups based on nature's most successful designs, Ken Thompson, Meghan-Kiffer Press, 2008

THE NETWORKED ENTERPRISE: Competing for the future through Virtual Enterprise Networks, Ken Thompson, Meghan-Kiffer Press, 2008

APPENDICES

A: XSim Business Acumen Simulation Game

XSim is a cloud-based business simulation played
in teams which at its medium level takes half a day and at
its advanced level takes a full day (or longer).

A typical *XSim* session involves 3-4 teams each with 4-6
participants. Each team will share a single computer
screen and a facilitator who will deliver key information as
well as listening to and offering feedback to both the team
and its members.

Xsim is aimed at managers and prospective managers and
is designed to touch all ten dilemmas described in this
book. The use of *Xsim* with the group is usually
customized in a prior planning session with the senior
learning sponsor to make sure it hits specific learning
objectives.

Xsim allows participants to be members of the business
unit leadership teams in a fictitious global Real-Time
Entertainment company called **NetBox**. **NetBox** is an
online video distributor for the latest movies, music and
sporting events.

The unique **NetBox** value proposition is "you only pay for
what you watch" where customers pay no subscription fees
and all revenue is based purely on the products consumed
in any quarter on a Pay As You Go (PAYG) basis.

A Systematic Guide to Business Acumen
and Leadership using Dilemmas

The aim of the simulation is for the team to achieve or exceed specific financial and non-financial targets over a full business year split into 4 quarters starting in January. Each quarter teams must react to both external changes in their markets and internal challenges in their enterprises by making decisions on pricing, product mix, operations, organizational health and special projects.

The simulation can be played in *competitive mode* or alternatively played in *collaborative mode* where the teams each represent different geographic business units operating within a single global corporation with both local and shared goals. The teams make all their decisions on a single dashboard as shown below.

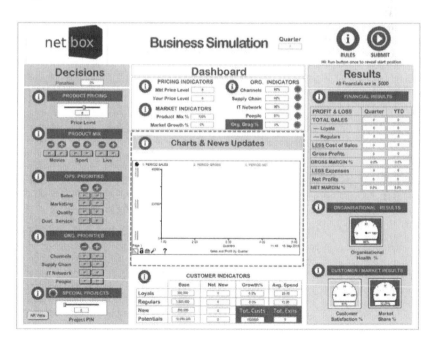

The simulation is supported by comprehensive set of briefing materials before and between rounds.

One of the most interesting aspects of it is the constant feeding of information to the team in the form of rumors and gossip some of which is important and some of it in the 'red herring' category. A collage of the different types of briefing materials in *Xsim* is shown below.

Simulation updates cover normal 'Business Turbulence' activities and when played in advanced mode also expose the participants to a full blown organization crisis which they must handle every round!

A Systematic Guide to Business Acumen and Leadership using Dilemmas

Developing your teams and leadership styles

A team-based simulation, such as Xsim, can be used not just develop understanding of business acumen but also to learn about team dynamics and individual leadership styles.

For more details, please see 'Appendix D: High Performing Teams in a hurry!'

For more information on Xsim: www.dashboardsimulations.com

B: High performance leadership - business game research

Over the last 7-8 years I have been running in-house business acumen simulation games with a number of major enterprises who form executive teams for a global enterprise for a three-year period over a single (intensive) day.

A large number of teams, of different levels of seniority, have fully completed the simulation games. Based on observing and analyzing performance in these games it seems that there are at least 6 critical differences between top performers and the rest in the areas of leadership and decision-making.

Finding 1: Top Performers avoided the "Presumption of change" trap.

Evidence for Finding 1: Even though the game starts with each team inheriting a business from the previous executive team 95% of the participants showed no curiosity regarding how successful the previous leadership team had been and why!

It is amazing that almost all new leaders focus on what they need to change but not what they need to preserve. What to change is only part of the challenge and for whatever reason (ego, identity, peer pressure...) showing a lack of respect for the previous team's achievements seems to be a good predictor of sub-optimal performance.

Finding 2: Top Performers suspended assumptions, thoroughly reviewed all available instructions/background research, and actively sought out any available expert input.

Evidence for Finding 2: Senior teams or functional experts generally did worse in the game than expected and junior teams/non-functional experts generally did better than expected.

As people become more experienced and competent they often become more fixed on their "Golden Rules" ("this always works" or "never do this"). Whilst Golden Rules are generally a good and necessary thing they can also close people down to a fresh examination of the facts available to them. In many cases the evidence that was available would have directly challenged these golden rules if it had been properly and objectively evaluated.

Finding 3: Top Performers rigorously followed the discipline of evidence-based decision-making.

Evidence for Finding 3: 90% of the teams made at least one critical decision which was based purely on hunches or past prejudices rather than any actual evidence.

Evidence-based decision-making is the discipline of supporting every key decision with a reference to one or more sources of written evidence of an objective nature. Ideally this evidence should be representative and quantitative, but it can also be purely anecdotal, provided it can be verified by a third party.

Finding 4: Top Performers were prepared to make painful choices and trade-offs on their priorities where necessary.

Evidence for Finding 4: Team performance was assessed against a balanced scorecard of 5 key indicators covering revenue, profits, market share, customer growth and organizational maturity. In no case did any single team ever perform better than all the other teams on all 5 of these indicators.

For example, in the game to build market share you may need to focus investment on new customers, but to build revenue you may need to focus on existing customers who spend more. In benign market conditions you might not need to make a conscious choice between these two, however, in difficult trading conditions it may simply not be possible to achieve both, and you have to make a choice. Top performing teams always seemed to have a clear hierarchy of priorities - "this first, then this second, then this third" - that guided their actions at critical points.

Finding 5: Top Performers displayed "coherence" of strategy and action.

Evidence for Finding 5: Over 85% of the teams accidentally took actions that were inconsistent with the strategies they had developed at the start of the game. When this was pointed out they almost always responded that they did not wish to change their strategies.

A key question in determining whether you really have a "strategy" is what you decided NOT to do! If you cannot answer this question, then you probably don't have a strategy and are navigating reactively in response to changing circumstances. This usually leads to "mission drift" and consequent underperformance.

Finding 6: Top Performers are open to collaboration, even with "competitors", and are always looking for advantage through "mutual learning alliances".

Evidence for Finding 6: Even though the teams were not explicitly competing against each other, within the game less than 10% of them entered into any dialogue whatsoever with the other teams to explore if they could legitimately help each other or share useful information/experiences.

As well as learning from your colleagues you can also learn from your external partners, customers, suppliers and even your competitors. For example, if you are building a new market it can be an excellent strategy to collaborate with competitors to help build something that will become worth fighting over later. If you operate by the mental model/golden rule that anyone who is not my friend must be my enemy, then you are handicapping your ability to learn faster than your competition, which, in the end, may be fatal for you in your market.

C: Ten Central Dilemmas in Business

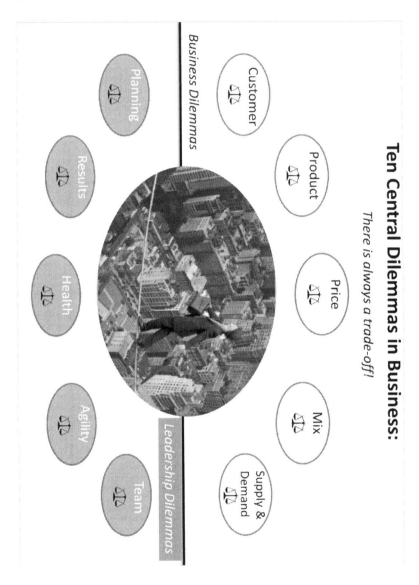

Ten Central Dilemmas in Business:

There is always a trade-off!

Business Dilemmas
- Planning
- Customer
- Results
- Product
- Health
- Price

Leadership Dilemmas
- Agility
- Mix
- Team
- Supply & Demand

D: High Performing Teams in a hurry!

Can you create a High-Performing Team in a day or afternoon or even over lunch? Of course not! However, if you are put in the position where you, as a leader, have to get the very best out of a group of colleagues in very short timescales what can you do?

Here is my 4-step approach to 'Instant Team'.

STEP1: Create Team 'Game Plan'

Below is my 7-point checklist which teams can use to produce a Team Game Plan (1-2 pages maximum):

1.   **R**oles
How will we divide up the team responsibilities?
2.   **A**greements (Ground Rules)
How will we deal with each other as colleagues and team members?
3.   **P**rocesses/Practices
What are the 2-3 most important team processes/practices will we put in place and follow?
4.   **P**riorities
How will we decide what is most important, particularly in dilemmas or under pressure? [2]
5.   **O**rganizational Values
What values are the most important to us as a team?
6.   **R**esults
What specific results must we achieve as our minimum team performance level?
7.   **T**argets
What is our 'stretch' target, our ambition to exceed our minimum performance level?

The first letter of each element spells 'R.A.P.P.O.R.T.' which is a useful mnemonic for a Team Game Plan. This is apt as 'Rapport' can be defined as '*A close and harmonious relationship in which the groups concerned understand each other's feelings or ideas and communicate well*' according to THE OXFORD DICTIONARY.

STEP 2: Test the Team

Do some short team-based activity as a Team and try to follow your Team Game Plan. You need to set aside at least 1 hour but 3 hours is better. If you have 3 hours, you can play a team-based business simulation or even some off-site activity. If you only have 1 hour you can still have a team problem-solving brainstorming meeting on a practical topic with which everyone is already familiar.

STEP 3: Reflect and Improve

At the end of this team activity, team members should take at least 30 minutes to discuss and reflect on a small number of key questions typically:

- How well are we working as a team – what could we improve?
- What would we do differently if we did the activity again?
- How closely are we following our team game plan – does this need to be revised?

If you have 2-3 hours, then you can conduct this review more than once as this allows the team to see visible improvements quickly. Another very useful device is to have the teams self-assess against the '*7 Mistakes Teams Make Under Pressure*' (see overleaf).

The '7 mistakes' have been gathered over ten years and represent the most common mistakes teams make participating in team-based business simulation games.

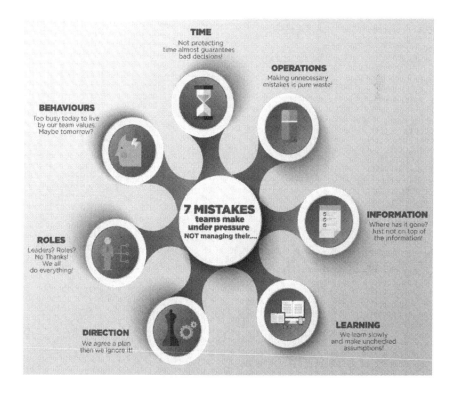

STEP 4: Execute and Review

Now you need to direct the team to the job in hand with the specific extra directive of 'Follow your Game Plan!' In addition, you must build in a regular (e.g. weekly) review cycle where you repeat the self-reflection/improvement from Step 4 using, of course, all the other guidance and tools offered in the rest of the book!

The Evolution of Team Working

If you observe newly formed and existing teams playing business simulations and other intensive challenges, you can gain some important insights into how team-working actually 'evolves'. This knowledge can help you accelerate the evolution of effective team working and collaboration in your own organizational teams.

On the road to Effective Team Collaboration there seems to be two intermediate phases of 'naïve collaboration' which teams often seem to go through - *Hyper-Communication* and *Over-Delegation*.

A Systematic Guide to Business Acumen and Leadership using Dilemmas

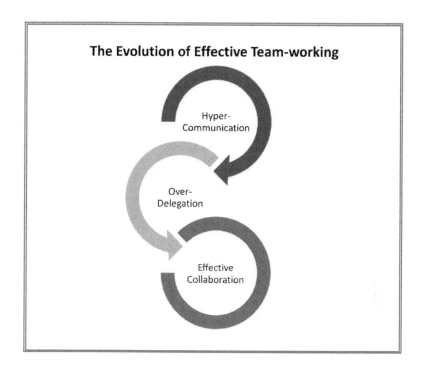

The Evolution of Effective Team-working

Hyper-Communication

Over-Delegation

Effective Collaboration

PHASE 1: Hyper-Communication

In this phase almost every team member is involved in almost every team conversation. It is very democratic and feels really good but the problem is that it just takes forever. A team operating like this will not hit its deadlines.

An organizational team meeting which conducts its Operational Meetings like this will not get through its agenda. In my experience teams usually start here on their journey towards effective collaboration. Teams in this phase genuinely believe that they are collaborating well UNTIL they suddenly discover that working like this is just not practical as it simply takes too long!

When teams have tried 'Hyper-Communication' they often *over-correct* and move to the next phase of naive collaboration: 'Over-Delegation'.

PHASE 2: Over-Delegation

In this phase the team quickly agree that they need to work faster and more efficiently. To achieve this, they wisely decide that they need some roles and division of labor but they 'over-delegate'. By this I mean they give out jobs to the different members and sub-teams but do not support this with sufficient communications to ensure they all stay on the same page.

Like the first phase, Hyper-Communication, teams think they have fixed their collaboration and they feel they are being very efficient UNTIL they discover, typically near the end of the round, that they are no longer all on the same page and that the team members have been working to different assumptions and priorities which invalidates much of their good work.

PHASE 3: Effective Collaboration

Once teams have experienced both of these naïve forms of collaboration (Hyper-Communication and Over-Delegation) they are well placed to find a middle ground with represents Effective Collaboration.

As with Over-Delegation they allocate roles but this time they also ensure that this is supported by on-going communications particularly around task objectives and early review of provisional findings/decisions before they become finalised.

Accelerated Team Development

From these insights it is clear that many teams find it very difficult to move directly into Effective Collaboration without first experiencing **and learning** from both Hyper-Communication and Over-Delegation.

I can't prove it but feel strongly that it may also be the case that many organisational teams simply *flip-flop* between the two naïve collaboration phases of Hyper-Communication and Over-Delegation without ever making the break-through into Effective Collaboration ... perhaps all the time believing, they are already doing it!

Therefore, to fast track effective team-working you need 3 simple ingredients:

1. **Mechanisms such as competitive business simulation games** or other short team challenges.

2. **Briefing for the teams on the challenges with specific deadlines and goals** but without any instruction about how they are to behave other than that they are a team.

3. **Facilitated team self-analysis sessions at the end of each round** or chunk of work to let teams review what kind of collaboration they are employing and how they might improve it.

If you carefully and skillfully work with these 3 ingredients, you can help teams in your organization develop effective team-working and collaboration skills in a much faster timescale than might be possible using other methods.

==
This section is a short extract from book 1 in The Systematic Guide series: 'A Systematic Guide to High Performing Teams (HPTs).
==

INDEX

Printed in Poland
by Amazon Fulfillment
Poland Sp. z o.o., Wrocław